MASTERS OF ART

VAN GOGH

ENRICA CRISPINO

♦

ILLUSTRATED BY
SIMONE BONI, FRANCESCA D'OTTAVI,
L.R. GALANTE, IVAN STALIO

PETER BEDRICK BOOKS
NEW YORK

DoGi

Produced by
Donati Giudici Associati, Florence
Original title:
*Van Gogh, l'esperienza straordinaria
del colore*
Text:
Enrica Crispino
Illustrations:
*Simone Boni, Francesca D'Ottavi,
L.R. Galante, Ivan Stalio*
Picture research and coordination of
co-editions:
Caroline Godard
Art direction:
*Oliviero Ciriaci
Sebastiano Ranchetti
Alessandro Rabatti*
Page design:
Sebastiano Ranchetti
Editing:
Enza Fontana
English translation:
Deborah Misuri-Charkham
Editor, English-language edition:
Ruth Nason
Typesetting:
Ken Alston – A.J. Latham Ltd

© 1996 Donati Giudici Associati s.r.l.
Florence, Italy

English language text © 1996 by
Macdonald Young Books/
Peter Bedrick Books
First published in the
United States of America
in 1996 by
Peter Bedrick Books
2112 Broadway
New York, NY 10023

ISBN 0-87226-525-0

Cataloging-in-Publication Data is
available for this book by request
from the Library of Congress,
Washington D.C., or from the
publisher.

Printed in 1996 by Amilcare Pizzi,
Cinisello Balsamo (Milan)

Photolitho:
Venanzoni DTP, Florence

♦ HOW THE INFORMATION IS PRESENTED

Every double-page spread is a chapter in its own right, devoted to an aspect of the life and art of Vincent van Gogh or the major artistic and cultural developments of his time. The text at the top of the left-hand page (1) and the large central illustration are concerned with this main theme. The text in italics (2) gives a chronological account of events in van Gogh's life. The other material (photographs, paintings and drawings) enlarges on the central theme.

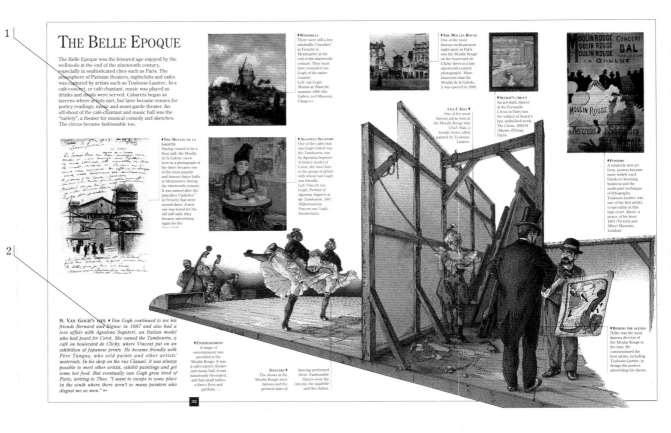

Some pages focus on major works by van Gogh. They include the following information: an account of the painting's history (1); a description of the content and imagery of the work (2); a critical analysis and detailed examination of its formal aspects (3). There are also reproductions of works by other artists, to set van Gogh's work in its historical context and demonstrate its originality.

CONTENTS

CONTEMPORARIES

Vincent van Gogh's life was brief and tormented. He could never achieve peace of mind and his relationships always failed. People who came into close contact with him found it hard to cope with his moods and strange behavior. This was the case even for those who most loved and admired him, such as his brother Theo and fellow artists Bernard and Gauguin. Yet, today, van Gogh is perhaps the most admired artist in the world. His paintings fetch the highest prices and exhibitions of his works attract record numbers of visitors. Without a doubt, van Gogh was one of the greatest and most innovative artists of the late nineteenth century: his many masterpieces, from *Bedroom in Arles* to *Starry Night*, are evidence of this. One of the new ideas that he introduced, which has most affected modern art, was that painting could express the feelings and inner world of the artist, rather than being an objective representation of the outside world. Van Gogh had links with all the original trends in art of his time, from Realism to Impressionism, from Seurat's Neo-Impressionism to the Synthetism of Bernard and Gauguin and the Expressionist movement, of which he has often been seen as a forerunner.

◆ **JULIEN TANGUY**
(1825-1894)
Père Tanguy, as his friends called him, had a shop in Paris selling paints. Artists of van Gogh's generation bought their materials from him.

◆ **EMILE BERNARD**
(1868-1941)
This French painter and important art theorist was one of the first people to recognize van Gogh' talent. He remained lifelong faithful friend.

CAMILLE PISSARRO ◆
(1830-1903)
One of the chief French Impressionists, Pissarro later also painted in the divisionist style. He and his son Lucien were friends of Theo and Vincent van Gogh. He introduced Vincent to Dr Gachet.

◆ **JEAN-FRANÇOIS MILLET**
(1814-1875)
Millet was a master of French realistic painting. His scenes of peasant life were one of van Gogh's artistic models.

◆ **GEORGES SEURAT**
(1859-1891)
The pioneer of divisionism, one of the great innovations in French painting, Seurat was a master whom van Gogh greatly admired.

VINCENT VAN GOGH ◆
(1853-1890)
Van Gogh's appearance is familiar to us because of his many self-portraits: red hair, often a short beard, bright and expressive eyes.

◆ **PAUL GAUGUIN**
(1848-1903)
Gauguin introduced a bold new decorative style of painting in the late nineteenth century. He moved from France to live in Polynesia.

HENRI DE ◆
TOULOUSE-LAUTREC
(1864-1901)
Paris nightlife was the subject of Lautrec's paintings. Two falls in his youth had stopped his legs from growing.

THEO VAN GOGH ♦
(1857-1891)
Theo was Vincent's favorite brother. He tried to help him in any way he could, and it was to him that Vincent wrote most of his letters. Theo was an art dealer. He married and had a son named after Vincent.

SIEN ♦
Clasina Maria Hoornik, known as Sien, was a prostitute in The Hague with whom van Gogh became involved. He took her to live with him, partly out of a feeling that she had been abandoned and needed someone to look after her, but the relationship ended after a year or so.

♦ JOSEPH ROULIN
A postal worker in Arles, Roulin was cheerful and unconventional and loved wine and became one of van Gogh's few real friends.

MARIE GINOUX ♦
Marie was the wife of Joseph Ginoux, who owned the café that van Gogh went to in Arles. She is the subject of a famous painting by van Gogh.

MINERS ♦
Van Gogh spent from 1878 to 1880 in the Belgian coalmining area of the Borinage. He went there as a preacher and devoted himself to alleviating the suffering of the miners, whose working and living conditions were appalling, and sharing their daily hardships.

PARENTS ♦
Van Gogh's father, Theodorus (1822-1885), was a Protestant minister. His mother, Anna Cornelia (1819-1907), was the daughter of a bookbinder in The Hague.

DOCTOR GACHET ♦
(1828-1909)
Paul-Ferdinand Gachet often invited van Gogh to his house in Auvers, near Paris, and helped him as a doctor in the last months of his life. He was friendly with artists such as Pissarro and Cézanne and himself painted as a hobby.

GROOT ZUNDERT

At the end of the nineteenth century, the inland regions of Holland remained untouched by the cultural interests, lively, tolerant atmosphere and openness to trade that had characterized Dutch coastal cities for centuries. It was in one of these inland regions, the province of Brabant, that Vincent van Gogh was born, son and grandson of Protestant clergymen. His background ensured that he came to hold deep religious beliefs, which lasted all his life, even though he became disillusioned and left the Church. There was, however, another family interest which, for Vincent, would become a passion: painting. Three of his uncles were art dealers and one of his mother's relations, Anton Mauve, was a leader of The Hague School of painting.

♦ **BRABANT**
In the nineteenth century the Dutch province of Brabant, on the country's border with Belgium, was predominantly agricultural. Its inhabitants were a mix of Catholics and Protestants. The region remained relatively backward at a time when Holland's industry was expanding and trade with the colonies in the East Indies was growing.

VINCENT'S PARENTS ♦
Theodorus van Gogh was the son of a Protestant pastor and became a pastor himself. He settled in the parish of Groot Zundert in 1849. Two years later, he married Anna Cornelia Carbentus. The couple's first child was still-born. Then Vincent was born and after him five others.

♦ **THE CHURCH AT NUENEN**
Since Vincent van Gogh grew up in a district where his father was a pastor, it is not surprising that churches were the subject of many of his early paintings. This one is entitled *Worshippers Leaving the Church at Nuenen*, January 1884 (Rijksmuseum Vincent van Gogh, Amsterdam). His father had moved to Nuenen in 1883.

♦ **ANTON MAUVE** (1838-1888)
Anton Mauve, a distant relation, gave Vincent some lessons in 1881-82. He was a member of The Hague School, an important group of Dutch artists in the late nineteenth century. These artists drew inspiration from the realistic style of the French Barbizon School, but also continued the realist tradition of seventeenth-century Dutch art.
Above: Anton Mauve, *The Seaweed Gatherer* (Musée d'Orsay, Paris).

♦ **THE CHURCH**
The parish of the church at Groot Zundert covered a large area, but the number of Protestants living there was quite small. The region was predominantly Catholic.

♦ **AGED THIRTEEN**
This photograph, taken in 1866, shows Vincent van Gogh as a thirteen-year-old boarder at Tilburg, near Zundert. He would leave school two years later.

♦ **AGED EIGHTEEN**
Van Gogh in 1871. He had been working for two years for a fine art dealer in The Hague, where he was able to draw, visit museums and study the history of art.

VAN GOGH'S LIFE

1. *Vincent's father, Theodorus van Gogh, was the Protestant pastor of Groot Zundert, a rural village in the province of Brabant, some 80 kilometers (50 miles) from Breda, in southern Holland. His mother, Anna Cornelia Carbentus, was the daughter of a bookbinder at the court of The Hague. Vincent was born on March 30, 1853, in the house next to the church at Zundert, and exactly one year after his older brother, also named Vincent, had died at birth. The next son, Theodorus, known as Theo, was born on May 1, 1857, and Vincent became very attached to him from the start. Vincent went to boarding school, near Zundert, but family finances soon made it necessary for him to leave and find a job.* ➡

LONDON

The 1870s, for Great Britain, were years marked by efforts to expand its empire to include Egypt, Afghanistan and South Africa. Queen Victoria became Empress of India in 1876, by which time the British Empire, protected by the Royal Navy, covered vast areas of the world. Rapid industrial development was also taking place, and so Britain was seen as the "workshop of the world". The other side of the coin was that millions of British working people were living at subsistence level, in poor and degrading conditions. In the poverty-stricken districts of London, hundreds of thousands of malnourished men, women and children were crowded into appallingly unhygienic housing. This was the London that Charles Dickens described in his novels. For some years, radical and Christian philanthropists had agitated to improve the conditions of the poor. Van Gogh came into contact with such people during his stay in England from 1873 to 1875.

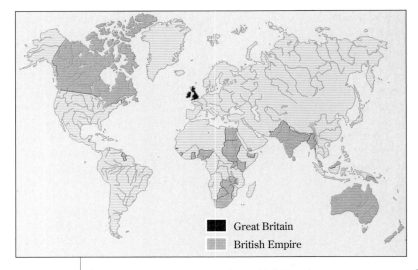

♦ **THE BRITISH EMPIRE**
During the last decades of the nineteenth century, the British Empire was by far the largest of all the empires built by European powers.

Great Britain

British Empire

♦ **QUEEN VICTORIA**
(1819-1901)
The niece of William IV, Victoria succeeded him to the British throne in 1837 and remained Queen until her death. She was a forthright character, who gave her name to the long period of British history known as the Victorian Age.
Left: *Portrait of Queen Victoria* by Edward M. Ward (Forbes Magazine Collection, New York).

MEANS OF ♦ TRANSPORT
At the end of the nineteenth century in London, goods were still transported by horse-drawn carts, while people needing to travel around could use the underground or electric trams. Motor vehicles did not become widespread, because, until 1896, English law set the speed limit at 6 kilometers (4 miles) per hour.

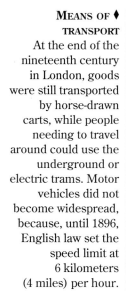

♦ WORKERS
Living conditions of workers were extremely poor and trade unionists began to agitate to demand more humane working hours and better working conditions in the factories.

♦ POVERTY
Britain's division between rich and poor was particularly obvious in London. In this richest city in the world, thousands of people suffered from malnutrition and lived in unhealthy dwellings.

♦ FROM ENGLAND
Vincent's letters to Theo are a mine of information about his life. In one dated April 1876, he included this sketch of Ramsgate, on the southeast coast of England (Rijks-museum Vincent van Gogh, Amsterdam). Vincent moved there after a few months' work in Paris.

♦ MYSTERY IN FACT AND FICTION
Between the summer and the start of winter in 1888, London was shocked by a series of savage murders. In some cases the murderer wrote a letter to the newspapers, saying when he would strike next. In total there were six victims of Jack the Ripper. Mysteries reigned in literature, too: in 1887, Arthur Conan Doyle began to write stories about Sherlock Holmes (right in this drawing), king of fictional detectives.

2. VAN GOGH'S LIFE ♦ *Van Gogh's Uncle Vincent was a partner in a firm of art dealers, Goupil and Co., whose head office was in Paris. In summer 1869 he found his nephew a job in Goupil's branch in The Hague and in 1873 Theo also joined Goupil's, in Brussels. Also in 1873, Vincent visited Paris for the first time, for a few days, and then went on to the London office. As he gained experience, his interest in art began to grow, and his job allowed him to broaden his knowledge. In London he would take long walks and make sketches of the city. He left his first accommodation, which was too expensive, to lodge with Mrs Loyer, a clergyman's widow. Soon he fell in love with her daughter, Eugénie, who was already engaged and firmly rejected him. Vincent became extremely downhearted, suffered from loneliness and increasingly turned to religion for consolation. He read the Bible zealously and often went to church.* ➤➤

REALISM

Between 1830 and 1860, in France, Realism became important in literature and in painting. Writers and artists in this new style took their subjects from everyday life, describing them realistically. Because of the progress that had been made in technology and medicine, people put great faith in science. Thinkers of the time put forward socialist ideas and positivist philosophies, the basis of which was that all meaningful knowledge came from what could be seen and experienced. The painters who turned towards Realism were rebelling against the art academies and against the belief that the most important art was that which represented historical and mythological subjects. The Barbizon School painted real landscapes, and artists such as Courbet and Millet portrayed ordinary people. Such paintings of people at work and simple woodland scenes were not easy for traditionalists to accept. But van Gogh had no doubts. He liked to paint peasant life and the artist he modeled himself on at first was Millet.

WORK ♦
Peasant life, farm work and the hardships suffered by ordinary city-dwellers became the subject-matter of Realist artists. Their paintings captured van Gogh's interest. 1. Honoré Daumier, *The Laundress*, 1860 (Musée d'Orsay, Paris); 2. Jean-François Millet, *The Gleaners*, 1857 (Musée d'Orsay, Paris); 3. Jules Breton, *The Return of the Gleaners*, detail, 1859 (Musée d'Orsay, Paris).

WOODLAND ♦
During the 1830s a group of landscape painters settled in the village of Barbizon, on the edge of the Forest of Fontainebleau. Woods and trees were the favorite subjects of Théodore Rousseau, Charles Daubigny and Jean-François Millet. 1.2.3. Gustave Courbet, *The Vercingetorix Oak*, 1864, details and complete (Pennsylvania Academy of Fine Arts, Philadelphia); 4. Théodore Rousseau, *Morning in the Forest of Fontainebleau*, 1850 (Wallace Collection, London); 5. Jean-François Millet, *Spring*, 1868-73 (Musée d'Orsay, Paris).

♦ EMILE ZOLA AND NATURALISM
The French novelist Emile Zola (1840-1902) led the Naturalist movement, which held that literature should describe life from an objective viewpoint, in "scientific" detail. He claimed that he put characters in a particular social setting and then studied the interaction between their temperament and the environment. Left: *Emile Zola*, by Manet, 1868, detail (Musée d'Orsay, Paris).

ANIMALS ♦
Rejecting the Romantic style of the earlier nineteenth century, the Realist painters, whether they belonged to the Barbizon School or followed Gustave Courbet, were interested in any subject taken from the natural world, including animals. 1. Constant Troyon, *The Pointer*, 1860 (Museum of Fine Arts, Boston); 2. Gustave Courbet, *Spring Mating Season*, 1861 (Musée d'Orsay, Paris).

♦ A SHOCKING PAINTING
Gustave Courbet (1819-1877) became the leader of the Realist movement in art.

His painting *Burial at Ornans*, 1849-50 (Musée d'Orsay, Paris), was exhibited at the Salon of 1850-51 and caused an uproar.

Never before had a scene with working people been presented in this way. Courbet had established a new kind of social art.

3. VAN GOGH'S LIFE ♦ *In a letter to Theo in January 1874, Vincent listed his favorite painters. He mentioned fifty-six, including Millet, Rousseau, Breton, Troyon and Mauve – all exponents of Realism. In 1875, he was transferred to Goupil's head office in Paris but seems to have neglected his duties as he became more and more deeply religious. On April 1, 1876, he was dismissed. He then returned to England, where he worked as a teacher, first in Ramsgate and then in the London suburb of Isleworth. Here, the headmaster, the Reverend Jones, also employed him as an assistant in his church. In December van Gogh returned to his parents' home: they had moved to the village of Etten, near Breda. In 1877 he started work in a Dordrecht bookshop but left for Amsterdam in May. His plans to study theology at the university there came to nothing.* ≫•

THE MINES

In the second half of the nineteenth century, Belgium was one of the world's largest producers of coal. The coalmines were the source of the country's wealth, thanks to advances in technology which had made it possible to increase production. The introduction of wheeled carts for transporting coal along underground tracks and steam-driven elevators for lifting it to the surface had somewhat improved working conditions in the mines, but, even so, a coal miner's life was still extremely hard. Van Gogh went as a lay preacher to the Belgian mining region of the Borinage, where he felt compelled to share the miners' living conditions. Men, women and children were forced to perform backbreaking tasks, in an unhealthy atmosphere where safety precautions were almost non-existent. They were paid a pittance and lived in squalid conditions.

♦ THE MINERS
The miners' poor living conditions were almost the only subject that van Gogh drew and painted when he was in the Borinage.
Left: *Return of the Miners*, 1880 (Rijksmuseum Kröller-Müller, Otterlo).

♦ THE COAL MERCHANT
Van Gogh included this drawing in a letter to Theo in November 1878 (Rijksmuseum Vincent van Gogh, Amsterdam).

LAMPS ♦
Firedamp present in the air in the mines was highly flammable and there was a danger of explosions if it came into contact with heat from candle or torch flames. Miners therefore had special lamps with a shield around the flame.

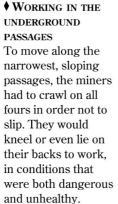

♦ WORKING IN THE UNDERGROUND PASSAGES

To move along the narrowest, sloping passages, the miners had to crawl on all fours in order not to slip. They would kneel or even lie on their backs to work, in conditions that were both dangerous and unhealthy.

♦ MANUAL LABOR

Even though new types of machinery were developed during the nineteenth century to improve productivity in the mines, the main work in the passageways cut in the coal veins was still done manually.

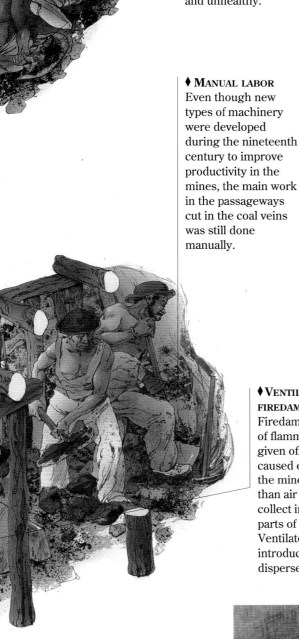

♦ VENTILATORS FOR FIREDAMP

Firedamp, a mixture of flammable gases given off by coal, often caused explosions in the mines. It is lighter than air and tends to collect in the upper parts of the mine. Ventilators were introduced to disperse it.

♦ ON THE SURFACE

Women and children made up a group of badly-paid, unskilled mine-workers. They were mainly used for tasks on the surface, such as breaking up large pieces of coal.

♦ COAL CARTS

Carts filled with coal ran along rails laid in the mine.

♦ UNDERGROUND

As soon as they went down into the mine, the coal miners were surrounded by darkness, which was broken only by the faint light of oil and benzine lamps.

♦ IN THE DEPTHS

When they reached depths of over 200 meters (650 feet), the miners had to work half-naked because of the heat.

A SHOVELLER ♦
After he left the Borinage, van Gogh continued to take an interest in the humblest of laborers.
Right: a drawing entitled *The Shoveller's Rest*, 1882 (Private collection).

4. VAN GOGH'S LIFE ♦ *In 1878, wishing to become a lay preacher, van Gogh enrolled in an evangelical training school near Brussels. He failed the course but went on his own initiative to work at Pâturages in the Borinage, a mining region in southern Belgium. The evangelical board relented and took him on for a six-month trial period. Now at Wasmes, he set himself to preach, to help the poor and to look after the sick. He threw himself into his work and wanted to identify with the people in his care. So, to share their experience, he lived in a hovel and slept on the ground. The board disapproved of this extreme way of life and dismissed him in July 1879. He stayed in the Borinage, however, working on his own at Cuesmes for a year. Before he left, he formed a new ambition: to become an artist. In 1880 he settled in Brussels where he made friends with the painter Anton van Rappard. His brother Theo was now sending him a little money.* ⇒▸

THE POTATO EATERS

The painting shown below is one of the many pictures of peasant life that van Gogh painted while he stayed with his parents in Nuenen. His father had moved to a new church there in 1883. In this case, he has portrayed a simple family scene. In a humble wooden house, five people seated around a table are having supper. In dim lamplight, some are helping themselves from a plate of boiled potatoes, an old man is drinking and an old woman is pouring coffee.

♦ THE LAMP
A detail from *The Potato Eaters*. The light cast by the lamp creates an intimate family atmosphere among the people seated at the table.

♦ THE WORK
The Potato Eaters, 1885, oil on canvas, 81.5 x 114.5 cm (32 x 45 in) (Rijksmuseum Vincent van Gogh, Amsterdam). Van Gogh's signature is legible on the canvas. He painted the picture in April-May 1885, at Nuenen, his father's new parish. It was the final version of a composition he had been working on for several months. At the end of December 1884, he had begun painting portraits of peasants in the area, with a view to producing a picture of a group in an indoor setting. From February 1885, he made drawings and paintings and then a lithograph of a group of people around a dish of potatoes. He described the progress of the composition in his letters to Theo: "I am totally involved in painting heads. I paint during the day, and draw at night. I have painted and drawn in this way at least thirty times ... even at night by lamplight, in the peasants' houses, until it's so dark that I can't see the paint on the palette. This is so that I can understand as much as possible about the effects of light at night, such as, for example, a great dark patch on the wall."

♦ FIVE PEASANTS
Van Gogh returned to the theme of *The Potato Eaters* in 1890, at Saint-Rémy, where he produced the drawing shown above (Rijksmuseum Vincent van Gogh, Amsterdam).

The Potato Eaters *was Vincent van Gogh's first masterpiece and it is very clear that the painting was inspired by his search for an expressive style. His idea was that painting should be more concerned with conveying mood and expressing the inner feeling of the subject, than with representing it in meticulous outward detail. Van Gogh was therefore far removed from the Dutch painting tradition which was based on precise, realistic detail and accurate portrayals. He was much more in tune with the Realist painters of the nineteenth century, who were mostly French but also included some Dutch artists such as Jozef Israëls. Unlike Israëls, however, van Gogh did not treat his subjects with piety, but portrayed their weatherbeaten, work-worn features plainly and honestly.*

♦ THE LITHOGRAPH
This is the lithograph that van Gogh made of *The Potato Eaters*, in April 1885 (Rijksmuseum Kröller-Müller, Otterlo).

♦ SIMPLE THINGS
Left and right: details from *The Potato Eaters*. Van Gogh's interest in the poor and his wish to make their everyday life the focus of his artistic efforts link his paintings with the work of novelists such as Emile Zola and Charles Dickens. These two were his favorite authors.

♦ MODELS
At Nuenen, van Gogh used local people as his models and some became his friends. In September 1885, however, rumor had it that he was the father of a child expected by a young peasant girl, Gordina de Groot. His resulting unpopularity, and the lack of models, were among the reasons why he left Nuenen. Left: *Head of a Peasant Woman*, 1885 (Rijksmuseum Vincent van Gogh, Amsterdam).

WORK ♦
Van Gogh did not idealize the peasants, but portrayed them as they really were. Right: *Peasant Woman with Spade*, August 1885 (Barber Institute of Fine Arts, Birmingham).

♦ THE PEASANT WOMAN
A detail from *The Potato Eaters*, 1885. In a letter to Theo in April 1885, Vincent wrote about the delicate colors that the wind and the sun produced on the peasant women's clothing. The colors he used at this time, however, were rather dark and earthy.

JOZEF ISRAËLS ♦
(1824-1911) Jozef Israëls was one of the leading members of The Hague School of painting during the second half of the nineteenth century. In contrast to Anton Mauve, he chose to paint urban subjects and family settings. He tended to portray people in a rather sentimental way. Right: Jozef Israëls, *Inside a Hovel*, detail, 1890 (Musée d'Orsay, Paris).

ANTWERP

Belgium gained independence from Holland in 1831 and, in the second half of the nineteenth century, became a prosperous and active nation even though there was rivalry between its Flemish and Walloon communities. The country's economy was built on coalmining, industrial expansion and the resources of its colonies. At the center of its system of production and trade was the port of Antwerp, a large Flemish city on the Schelde, 90 kilometers (56 miles) from the North Sea. Goods and commodities poured into Antwerp from America, Asia and other parts of the world. Information and ideas from different cultures, including Japan, also flowed in, creating a cosmopolitan atmosphere. However, Antwerp in the nineteenth century did not quite achieve the cultural heights it had reached during the seventeenth century, when it had been home to the great Flemish Baroque painter Peter Paul Rubens.

♦ **VAN GOGH AND JAPAN**
Many Japanese color prints were among the more exotic goods arriving in the port of Antwerp. It was when he was in this city that van Gogh first saw examples of them. When he moved to Paris, he had the opportunity to increase his knowledge of Japanese art. He used some Japanese prints in the background of his *Portrait of Père Tanguy* (left), autumn, 1887 (Musée Rodin, Paris).

♦ **MANET AND JAPAN**
The Impressionist Edouard Manet was one of the first European painters to take an interest in Japanese art. In his *Portrait of Emile Zola* (above), 1868 (Musée d'Orsay, Paris), he included a print by the Japanese artist Kuniaki, in the background on the right; and a Japanese screen on the left.

THE STADHUIS ♦
The Stadhuis (town hall) was on the main square in the center of Antwerp. Van Gogh made a drawing of it.

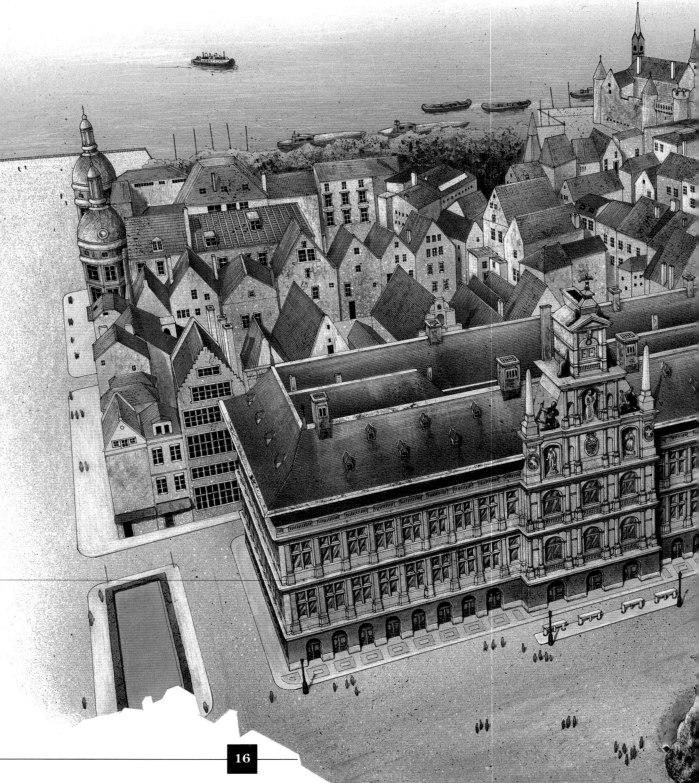

THE PORT ♦
Van Gogh moved to Antwerp from rural Nuenen. Living in this lively, cosmopolitan city was some preparation for his next move, to Paris. In Antwerp he produced paintings such as *View of the Port of Antwerp*, 1885 (Rijksmuseum Vincent van Gogh, Amsterdam).

 ♦ RUBENS
During the three months he spent in Antwerp, van Gogh studied the works of the Flemish master Peter Paul Rubens and developed a great admiration for this artist. In addition, he secured admission to the city's Art Academy, to improve his technical skill as an artist.
Left: Peter Paul Rubens, *Self-portrait with his Wife, Isabella Brant*, 1609-10 (Alte Pinakothek, Munich).

♦ THE SCHELDE
The port of Antwerp grew up on the estuary of the river Schelde, some 90 kilometers (56 miles) from the sea. It was Belgium's largest port and one of the main ports in Europe.

♦ GUILDHALLS
On the main square were the premises of the old guilds, such as those of coopers, haberdashers and wool-makers. Guilds had been powerful in this city where trade was the main occupation.

♦ HIROSHIGE
One of the greatest Japanese artists of the nineteenth century, whose work also came to be appreciated in the West, was Ando Hiroshige (1797-1858).
Left: *The Bridge of Kyoto by the Light of the Moon*, a print by Hiroshige taken from *One Hundred Views of Edo* (1856-59).

5. VAN GOGH'S LIFE ♦ *In 1882 van Gogh was in The Hague, where he painted and developed a relationship with a prostitute known as Sien. For a while he lived with her and thought of marrying her, but eventually he put his artistic career first and they parted in 1883. After spending some time in the province of Drenthe, he moved south to Nuenen in Brabant, where his father now had his parish. During the next two years he produced hundreds of paintings and drawings of the local peasant community. He also read, took piano lessons, and even gave painting lessons to amateur artists. His father died in March 1885 and the local people turned against him. He was falsely accused of fathering the child of a peasant girl whom he had used as a model. In November he moved to Antwerp, where he lodged in a room above an art materials shop. He visited museums to see the works of Rubens. He read Zola, discovered Japanese prints (using them to decorate the walls of his room) and enrolled in the Art Academy. He was never to return to Holland.* ⟫

STILL LIFE

This painting of 1885 shows a seemingly haphazard collection of everyday objects: a straw hat, a meerschaum pipe, a bottle and some containers. As we shall see, however, these are all objects which reappear in a number of van Gogh's paintings, sometimes in connection with a human figure and sometimes not. They were used by van Gogh to study the effects of light and this particular painting probably served as a visual aid in the painting classes he gave while he was in Nuenen.

♦ FAMILIAR OBJECTS
Van Gogh made many drawings of everyday objects in 1885 (Rijksmuseum Vincent van Gogh, Amsterdam).

THE BOTTLE ♦
A detail from *Still Life with Straw Hat*. It was while he was staying in Nuenen that van Gogh began his lengthy research into color. From then, his paintings were often based on the way colors look under different light conditions.

♦ THE WORK
Still Life with Straw Hat, 1885, oil on canvas, 36 x 53.5 cm (14 x 21 in) (Rijksmuseum Kröller-Müller, Otterlo). The work was painted during the spring-summer of 1885, when van Gogh was still at Nuenen. Although most of his output during this period consisted of portraits of peasants at work and landscape scenes, he also made many studies of birds' nests and other objects.

During the period when he was living in Nuenen (1883-1885), van Gogh decided to begin his own, personal study of light and color. The letters he wrote to his brother Theo at this time contain meticulous notes on how to create a certain color and on the reaction of colors to light. He was excited by seeing works by Rembrandt, Rubens and Frans Hals. In a letter written in mid-October 1885, he considered the use of black: "Can you use black and white, or not? ... Frans Hals uses no fewer than twenty-seven blacks." He concluded: "Black and white have a meaning of their own, and it is a mistake to try to avoid using them." Above all, however, van Gogh was interested in light and the range of colors that he used in his paintings now became markedly brighter.

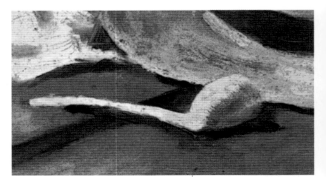

♦ THE PIPE
A detail from *Still Life with Straw Hat*. Van Gogh was never separated from his pipe and it often appears in his paintings.

♦ JUST A BRUSH-STROKE
Left: a detail from *Still Life with Straw Hat.* Right: a detail from *Still Life with Clogs.* Both these details show the same technique: the effect of light catching on an object is conveyed by brush-strokes in a paler shade of the color used for the object. The result is that the object stands out clearly from the dark monochrome of the background.

♦ LESSONS FROM THE MASTERS
Frans Hals, Rubens and Rembrandt were among the accepted Dutch and Flemish masters whose paintings van Gogh most admired. "Frans Hals," he wrote, "is a colorist among colorists ... like Veronese, Rubens, Delacroix, Velázquez. It has been quite rightly said that Millet, Rembrandt and, for example, Israëls are more harmonizers than colorists."
Above: Hals, *Banquet of the Officers of the Militia Company of St George,* 1616, detail (Frans Halsmuseum, Haarlem).

CLOGS ♦
In the period just before he left Holland for good, van Gogh painted a series of still lifes. Above: *Still Life with Clogs,* (Rijksmuseum Kröller-Müller, Otterlo), like *Still Life with Straw Hat,* was painted in mid-1885. Again, in this painting, van Gogh was furthering his study of light and color. He wanted to investigate the possibilities of dark colors.

♦ OBJECTS AND SYMBOLS
Left: *Still Life with Bible* (Rijksmuseum Vincent van Gogh, Amsterdam) was painted in April 1885. Van Gogh placed symbolic meaning on the everyday objects in this composition. The open Bible represents his father, who had died the previous month. The well-worn copy of Emile Zola's novel *Joie de Vivre* symbolizes Vincent himself.

THEO VAN GOGH

Theo van Gogh was Vincent's favorite brother and, between August 1872 and 27 July 1890, was the main and often the only person to whom Vincent wrote. In his letters, the artist told Theo about his problems and plans and asked for his reactions, which were at times very critical, to his own ideas. Their relationship was close and strong, with Theo not only in the role of confidant but also serving as art expert – he was the manager of an art dealer's – and providing financial help. Theo's profession was one that had arisen from the success of the many art galleries which opened during the second half of the nineteenth century, particularly in Paris.

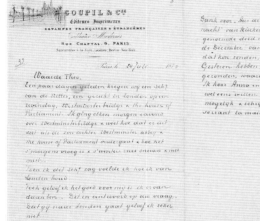

◆ **THE YOUNGER BROTHER**
Above: a photograph of Theo van Gogh (Rijksmuseum Vincent van Gogh, Amsterdam). Theo was born in Groot Zundert on May 1, 1857, and was the third of six brothers and sisters. He was four years younger than Vincent. In 1889, he married Johanna Bonger. Their son, whom they called Vincent, was born in 1890. Theo died on January 25, 1891, soon after his older brother.

◆ **DEAR THEO**
The letters that Vincent van Gogh wrote have provided information and helped to explain his complex personality, his ideas and his artistic aims and opinions. Of the 821 letters that he wrote, 668 were to Theo. The one reproduced above, written on Goupil's headed notepaper and dated 24 July 1875, was sent from London. Many of the letters also contained rough sketches, portraits, and plans and copies of paintings.

BOUSSOD AND VALADON ◆
The small gallery managed by Theo was one of many that had opened in Paris in the last decades of the nineteenth century. It was a branch of what had been Goupil's, located at 19 boulevard Montmartre. By Theo's time it was Boussod and Valadon.

6. VAN GOGH'S LIFE ◆ *Van Gogh took courses at the Art Academy in Antwerp, even studying at night, but despite these efforts he was still considered "unsuitable" to proceed to the next level of tuition. He had argued with some of the conventional teaching. He did not wait for official notification of his examination results and left for Paris. He arrived there unexpectedly on February 28, 1886, and sent a note to his brother Theo, who met him at the Louvre. At that time, Theo was busily involved in running the Boussod and Valadon gallery and he would really have preferred Vincent to return home to their mother in Brabant. He tried to persuade him to do so, but Vincent remained obstinate that he would stay. Theo continued to be his one true support, both financially and morally.* ➡➤

GROUND FLOOR ◆
What was popular on the Paris art market or at least among the clients of Boussod and Valadon was not necessarily what Theo most liked. He preferred the works of the Impressionists. In the gallery he managed, he was obliged to give pride of place on the ground floor to traditional painters. Bouguereau was the one who enjoyed the greatest commercial success.

♦ MEZZANINE
Theo used the
mezzanine of his
gallery to show
paintings by Corot,
Daumier, Manet,
Renoir, Monet and, in
particular, Degas to
his more
sophisticated clients.

♦ THE ART DEALER
Theo van Gogh
stayed with the art-
dealing company,
Goupil's, all his
working life. He spent
time in the branches
in Brussels and
The Hague (above)
and finally moved
to Paris.

He had a very open
mind when
considering the work
of contemporary
artists and was one of
the first people to
appreciate the value
of his brother
Vincent's work. He
tried, with little
success, to sell it.

PARIS IN 1886

When Vincent van Gogh arrived in Paris in 1886, the art world was beginning to recognize the importance of the controversial new paintings that had appeared in previous years. The Impressionists were holding their eighth and last exhibition, but some of the movement's best-known members, including Renoir and Monet, had refused to show their work. Two newcomers, Seurat and Signac, along with Pissarro, showed pictures at the exhibition in a new style now often known as "Neo-Impressionist". Other names for it, based on the technique employed, were "divisionist" and "pointillist". The variety of artistic styles was gradually increasing, with new figures on the scene such as Odilon Redon, Paul Gauguin, the Italian Giovanni Boldini and the eccentric Henri Rousseau, called "le Douanier Rousseau" because he worked for the Paris customs office.

♦ **THE CORMON ATELIER**
One of the most prestigious places to study in Paris was the studio of Fernand Cormon. He was a very successful, though conventional painter and a good teacher. In his studio (shown above in a photograph of 1886) van Gogh met Bernard, Anquetin and Toulouse-Lautrec.

7. VAN GOGH'S LIFE ♦ *Vincent shared Theo's apartment in the rue Laval (now rue Victor-Massé), not too far from the gallery that his brother managed. In June 1886, they moved to a larger apartment in the rue Lepic. Vincent was determined to make the most of Paris. He painted furiously, met many fellow artists and studied at the Cormon atelier, one of the city's best-known teaching studios. Theo put up with his brother's unpredictable mood-swings and wrote: "It's as if he were two completely different people. One is sweet, sensitive and extraordinarily gifted; the other egotistical and hard-hearted." Meanwhile their mother moved away from Nuenen and many of Vincent's works, left behind there, were lost as a result.* ➤

THE IMPRESSIONISTS ♦
By 1886 the Impressionists were winning their battle and the value of their work had begun to be recognized.

1. Claude Monet, *Woman with Parasol*, detail, 1886 (Musée d'Orsay, Paris); 2. Edgar Degas, *The Tub*, 1886 (Musée d'Orsay, Paris); 3. Pierre-Auguste Renoir, *The Great Bathers*, 1884-87 (Museum of Art, Philadelphia).

THE DIVISIONISTS ♦
The most innovative works at the 1886 Impressionist exhibition were those of the divisionist painters, who are also called pointillists or Neo-Impressionists. Seurat's *La Grande Jatte* caused a sensation.

1. Camille Pissarro, *The Gleaners*, detail, 1889 (Öffentliche Kunstsammlung, Basel); 2. Georges Seurat, *La Grande Jatte*, 1884-86 (Art Institute, Chicago); 3. Paul Signac, *The Dining Room*, detail, 1886-87 (Rijksmuseum Kröller-Müller, Otterlo).

NEW ARTISTS ♦
Henri Rousseau (1844-1910), known as Le Douanier, and the Italian Giovanni Boldini (1842-1931) were among the new artists to emerge in Paris in the 1880s and 1890s.

1. Giovanni Boldini, *Portrait of Giuseppe Verdi*, 1886 (Galleria Nazionale di Arte Moderna, Rome); 2. Henri Rousseau, *Carnival Night*, detail, 1886 (Museum of Art, Philadelphia); 3. Henri Rousseau, *A Riverbank*, 1886 (Private collection, Paris).

THE EIFFEL TOWER

From 1851 onwards, exhibitions of manufactures and crafts from around the world were held periodically in the capital cities of Europe and America. People visiting the huge International Exhibitions, or World Fairs, held in London, New York and Paris could see the material results of the faith that had been placed in science and view the latest developments in technology. When van Gogh arrived in Paris in 1886, the city was already preparing for the International Exhibition that was to be held there in 1889, to celebrate the centenary of the French Revolution. The Eiffel Tower was built as a gateway to the Exhibition; it became a permanent symbol of the French capital.

♦ **EIFFEL, THE ENGINEER** (1832-1923) Alexandre-Gustave Eiffel was a great engineer and entrepreneur. A specialist in building work using iron and steel, he had also designed the steel framework for the Statue of Liberty in New York Harbor. Left: a portrait by Viesseux (Musée d'Orsay, Paris).

A WONDER ♦ OF TECHNOLOGY The pieces of iron from which the tower was built were prepared in a machine shop, with great accuracy, and then put together, on site, by small teams of specialist workers.

♦ **THE FINISHED TOWER** The tower weighs about 9,500,000 kilograms (9,350 tons). Its four uprights merge and rise to a height of 300 meters (984 feet) and it has three platforms, with restaurants and offices. The tower was ready for the opening of the International Exhibition on March 31, 1889, though the third platform was not added until May.

♦ **A PUBLIC SUCCESS** The International Exhibition lasted 173 days, during which time 1,900,000 people visited the Eiffel Tower. Four staircases, with a total of 1,792 steps, led to the uppermost platform. Eiffel had a lavishly decorated office at the top of the tower which he also used as a laboratory for studying aerodynamics, astronomy and meteorology.

PAINTINGS OF THE ♦ TOWER

Some sections of intellectual society were critical of the tower, but there were many artists who did not share this view. They were happy to include the tower in their paintings of the city.
Right: a detail from Henri Rousseau's *Self-portrait – Landscape*, 1889-90 (Národni Galerie, Prague).

♦ POSTERS OF THE ♦ TOWER

Many posters were printed to mark the opening of the Eiffel Tower in 1889. The International Exhibition was a spectacular and cosmopolitan event, and its success helped France's recovery after the country's traumatic defeat by Prussia nineteen years earlier.

♦ THE UPRIGHTS

The tower is supported by four uprights and each of these has its own elevator which ascends on a curve. Two of them go to the first platform and two to the second. A fifth travels the 78 meters (256 feet) between the second and third levels.

♦ WOODEN SUPPORTS

Building such a tall metal structure was an extraordinary undertaking. Huge wooden supports were needed when work began. Once the first platform had been completed, the wooden structures were dismantled.

♦ PRAISE AND CRITICISM

After the tower had been built, Gustave Eiffel was decorated with France's highest award, the Legion of Honor, while a large number of writers, artists and musicians "protested with all their strength and with all their indignation, in the name of French taste which had been disregarded" against the building of the "useless and monstrous Eiffel Tower" in the heart of the city. In response to these criticisms, Eiffel wrote an article claiming that the tower had an abstract beauty of its own. It was, he said, the product of logic and science and its very existence was a "symbol of man's victory over the problems imposed by the laws of nature".

ASNIÈRES

The small Parisian suburb of Asnières, with its bridges over the Seine, fishing boats moored along the riverbanks, tree-lined avenues and cafés, had already been the setting of many Impressionist paintings. Monet, Pissarro, Renoir and Caillebotte had all found that Asnières had the right atmosphere for painting "en plein air" (in the open). Van Gogh followed in their footsteps. In the painting shown here, he captured one of the best-known views of Asnières: a spot where the river was crossed by a series of arched bridges. One of the bridges was for the railway.

♦ **BERNARD'S VIEW OF ASNIÈRES**
Emile Bernard also painted *Bridges at Asnières* (Museum of Modern Art, New York) during the summer of 1887.

♦ **THE WORK**
Bridges at Asnières, 1887, oil on canvas, 52 x 65 cm (20½ x 25½ in) (Bührle Collection, Zurich). Van Gogh painted this work during the summer of 1887 in Asnières, a suburb of Paris that he had discovered thanks to Emile Bernard (1868-1941).
Bernard was an intelligent and highly talented young artist and friend of Paul Gauguin, and he and van Gogh had met in 1886 in Fernand Cormon's studio, where they were both studying painting.
During his stay in Paris, Vincent often accompanied Bernard to Asnières, to paint "en plein air" as the Impressionists had done. Over a period of two years, van Gogh painted many versions of the bridges that cross the river there.

♦ **SOLITARY FIGURES**
Above and below: details from *Bridges at Asnières*.

"While painting at Asnières, I saw more colors than I have ever seen before." Behind these words of van Gogh is the sense that he was trying to get close to Impressionism. He studied the same techniques, chose the same subjects and went to the same places as the Impressionists had done.

He painted constantly, to try to acquire the ability they had to convey the quality of the atmosphere and light by the use of color. He changed from his original tendency towards Realism and was attracted instead by the idea of capturing fleeting impressions by working rapidly on the spot.

♦ **WITH BERNARD IN ASNIÈRES**
Bernard and van Gogh (with his back turned) talking by the Seine in 1886.

♦ **RAPID STROKES**
The banks of the Seine were often the subject of van Gogh's works as he tried to master the Impressionist technique. In this painting of the *Riverbank at Asnières*, 1887 (Rijksmuseum Vincent van Gogh, Amsterdam), the artist clearly tried to create the atmosphere by using short and rapid strokes of color.

A PERIOD OF STUDY ♦
The two years from 1886 to 1888 in Paris were a period of study for van Gogh. Thanks to his brother's contacts, he was also able to meet many of the most important contemporary artists. Vincent painted constantly and, although he showed a distinct preference for landscape painting – and for countryside rather than urban scenes – he did not neglect to practice in other fields of art, such as still life and portrait-painting. The greatest changes in his work at this time can be seen mainly in the views and still lifes that he produced: he now used lighter colors.

♦ **IMPRESSIONIST SUBJECTS AND TECHNIQUES**
Above and below: details from *Bridges at Asnières* show van Gogh's use of pure colors applied with rapid and short brush-strokes. The effect achieved by this technique is dynamic. The train introduces a modern theme into the natural surroundings.

Above right: *Still Life with Lemons*, 1887 (Rijksmuseum Vincent van Gogh, Amsterdam).
Right: *Portrait of the Art Dealer Alexander Reid*, 1887 (Art Gallery and Museum, Glasgow).

THE DIVISIONISTS

At the eighth Impressionist exhibition in Paris in 1886, the most innovative works were those of the divisionists. Seurat's *La Grande Jatte* caused a sensation. Instead of mixing colors on his palette, the artist had applied small dots of pure colors to the canvas, so that, seen from a distance, these colors blended (optical mixing). The French critic Félix Fénéon coined the word "pointillism" to describe this painting technique and called the artists who used it "Neo-Impressionists", but Seurat preferred the term "divisionism". The divisionists had carried further the Impressionists' study of light effects. Pissarro said that the "romantic" and "scientific" Impressionists had now parted company.

♦ SEURAT AND CHEVREUL'S WHEEL
Georges Seurat took an interest in scientific works and Eugène Chevreul's studies, published in 1839, had a fundamental influence on his own artistic development. In particular, Seurat used Chevreul's color wheel, which provided vital clues to the use of complementary colors, for example demonstrating that every color tends to introduce a tint of its complementary color into weaker colors next to it.

♦ GEORGES SEURAT
(1859-1891)
Coming from an upper middle-class family in Paris, Seurat was able to set up his own studio in 1872. He studied the painting of Piero della Francesca, and the work of other classical artists, with great enthusiasm, and also took a keen interest in reading scientific treatises. He worked tirelessly on his great compositions. First he made notes from life, including studies of colors recorded in black and white, and then he spent a great deal of time in his studio, painting. He was a strong personality who attracted a considerable following, even at his young age.
A sudden illness ended his short life on March 29, 1891, and so his last masterpiece, *The Circus*, was left unfinished.

8. VAN GOGH'S LIFE ♦ *Van Gogh attended the studio of Fernand Cormon, hoping that the master would help him to improve his technique. In fact, the main benefit of working there proved to be that he met a number of young artists such as Emile Bernard, Henri de Toulouse-Lautrec and Louis Anquetin. He made other contacts through his brother Theo. Despite the Boussod and Valadon directors, who disapproved of unconventional works, Theo set himself to promote Impressionist painting and other new trends in art. He introduced Vincent to the great Impressionist figures, Monet, Pissarro, Sisley and Renoir, and to younger innovators such as Signac and Seurat.* ➤➤

♦ THE CIRCUS PARADE
Above and left: details from Georges Seurat's *The Circus Parade*, 1887-88 (Metropolitan Museum, New York). Seurat was the artist who used the divisionist style most rigorously. In this painting, the colored dots are arranged in such a way that they create a halo effect around the figures.

♦ PAUL SIGNAC
(1863-1935)
From 1891, Paul Signac replaced his friend Seurat as leader of the Neo-Impressionist group. He came from a well-to-do family and was a frequent visitor to fashionable beach resorts in the south of France. From the time he met Seurat in 1884, he consistently adopted the divisionist technique.

Left: *The Lighthouse at Portrieux*, 1888 (Private collection); and below: a detail from the painting.

♦ DOTS OF COLOR
Divisionism, or pointillism, is a painting technique in which regular dots of pure color are applied with small brush-strokes. The term "divisionism" came from the fact that different colors of paint were kept separate or "divided". Most nineteenth-century painters mixed their colors on the palette. The Impressionists used various dabs, strokes or dots of pure color, but in spontaneous, unplanned fashion. Then Seurat produced the "scientific" version known as divisionism.

The works reproduced here help to explain the technique. Dots of pure colors were applied separately to the canvas, but when the picture is viewed from a distance, those colors combine on the retina of the viewer's eye. The effect is that the painting looks bright and luminous. Another divisionist feature is a kind of dotted frame around the picture. This serves to blend the colors of the painting with the color of the mount or frame chosen for it. Divisionist ideas were based on the findings of nineteenth-century scientists studying optics. One of these was the Frenchman Eugène Chevreul (1786-1889), photographed (above) on his one hundredth birthday by the famous Nadar.

MAXIMILIEN LUCE ♦
Right: *Paris from Montmartre*, 1887 (Musée du Petit Palais, Geneva) by the Parisian Maximilien Luce (1858-1941); and above: a detail of the painting.
Luce became a divisionist after Seurat's success in 1886-87. However, his interpretation of the divisionist method was less strict than Seurat's. His dots are distributed more freely and the colors less "scientifically" juxtaposed. Luce was deeply committed to contemporary social protest movements and most of his paintings concentrate on the life of the working classes. The painting shown here is an exception.

BOULEVARD DE CLICHY

Van Gogh preferred the countryside to the city. He did not even like Paris, one of the favorite subjects of painters such as Pissarro, Degas and Monet. Nonetheless, in his desire to master Impressionist and Neo-Impressionist techniques, he often devoted himself to portraying urban scenes such as this: a corner of a boulevard with a few cold passers-by enveloped in a grey light.

♦ **DETAILS OF THE BOULEVARD**
Above and below: details from *Boulevard de Clichy*.

♦ **THE OTHER FACE OF MONTMARTRE**
In *Vegetable Gardens in Montmartre*, 1887

(Stedelijk Museum, Amsterdam), van Gogh showed the area's rural side.

♦ **THE WORK**
Boulevard de Clichy, 1887, oil on canvas, 46.5 x 55 cm (18 x 21 in) (Rijksmuseum Vincent van Gogh, Amsterdam). The painting dates from February-March 1887. Van Gogh preferred the spaciousness of the Seine at Asnières, and the light and air of the open countryside, to built-up city surroundings. However, he did not neglect to paint urban subjects. The boulevard de Clichy lay at the foot of hilly Montmartre, not far from the apartment that he shared with his brother Theo. To produce works like this one, Vincent usually sketched the scene on site, making notes about the colors he would use when painting the final version.

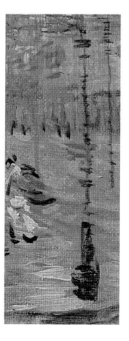

Cityscapes – images of modern daily life – were one of the favorite subjects of the Impressionist painters. Van Gogh also took up the challenge of painting the city, including the lively district of Montmartre, full of cafés and inhabited by artists. However, he preferred its more rural areas, where the city ended and *vegetable gardens began. It is evident from some works from this period that van Gogh was trying to master the techniques of the divisionists, using pure, unmixed colors and small brush-strokes. But he was too much an individualist to accept the divisionist discipline and adapted the method to his own type of expression.*

♦ **A STUDY**
A preparatory drawing for *Boulevard de Clichy*,

early 1887 (Rijksmuseum Vincent van Gogh, Amsterdam).

◆ A PERIOD OF
STUDY
These details from
Boulevard de Clichy
show that, by early
1887, van Gogh had
already learned a
great deal from his
time in Paris. A few
brush-strokes create
the impression of a
human figure (left)
or a tree (right). The
colors are pure and
much lighter than
the earthy tones of
his early works.

◆ ASNIÈRES AGAIN
With the onset of
better weather, van
Gogh left the city to
paint "en plein air" in
the countryside.
*Restaurant "La
Sirène"* (Musée
d'Orsay, Paris) was
painted in Asnières
during the summer
of 1887, and shows
how far van Gogh's
use of Impressionist
techniques had
advanced.

◆ VASES OF FLOWERS
This detail from
*Interior of a
Restaurant* shows how
van Gogh interpreted
divisionism: he
combined different
types of brush-stroke
with the dots of color,
producing a less
meticulous but more
vital result.

FOLLOWING SEURAT ◆
*Interior of a
Restaurant*, summer
1887 (Rijksmuseum
Kröller-Müller,
Otterlo), was as close
as van Gogh came to
the divisionism of
Seurat and Signac.
Using this technique
took time, for it
required meticulous
work. Van Gogh, on
the other hand,
wanted to express
himself quickly.

THE BELLE EPOQUE

The Belle Epoque was the leisured age enjoyed by the well-to-do at the end of the nineteenth century, especially in sophisticated cites such as Paris. The atmosphere of Parisian theaters, nightclubs and cafés was captured by artists such as Toulouse-Lautrec. In a café-concert, or café-chantant, music was played as drinks and meals were served. Cabarets began as taverns where artists met, but later became venues for poetry readings, music and avant-garde theater. An off-shoot of the café-chantant and music hall was the "variety", a theater for musical comedy and sketches. The circus became fashionable too.

♦ **WINDMILLS**
There were still a few windmills ("moulins" in French) in Montmartre at the end of the nineteenth century. They must have reminded van Gogh of his native country.
Left: van Gogh, *Moulin de Blute-fin*, summer 1886 (Art Gallery and Museum, Glasgow).

♦ **THE MOULIN DE LA GALETTE**
Having ceased to be a flour mill, the Moulin de la Galette (seen here in a photograph of the time) became one of the most popular and famous dance halls in Montmartre during the nineteenth century. It was named after the pancakes ("galettes" in French) that were served there. A new use was found for the old mill sails: they became advertising signs for the dance hall.

♦ **AGOSTINA SEGATORI**
One of the cafés that van Gogh visited was the Tambourin, run by Agostina Segatori. A former model of Corot, she was close to the group of artists with whom van Gogh was friendly.
Left: Vincent van Gogh, *Portrait of Agostina Segatori at the Tambourin*, 1887 (Rijksmuseum Vincent van Gogh, Amsterdam).

9. VAN GOGH'S LIFE ♦ *Van Gogh continued to see his friends Bernard and Signac in 1887 and also had a love affair with Agostina Segatori, an Italian model who had posed for Corot. She owned the Tambourin, a café on boulevard de Clichy, where Vincent put on an exhibition of Japanese prints. He became friendly with Père Tanguy, who sold paints and other artists' materials. In his shop on the rue Clauzel, it was always possible to meet other artists, exhibit paintings and get some hot food. But eventually van Gogh grew tired of Paris, writing to Theo: "I want to escape to some place in the south where there aren't so many painters who disgust me as men."* ⇒

♦ **ENTERTAINMENT**
A range of entertainment was provided at the Moulin Rouge. It was a café-concert, theater and music hall. It was luxuriously decorated, and had small tables, a dance floor and gardens.

DANCERS ♦
The shows at the Moulin Rouge were famous and the greatest stars of dancing performed there. Fashionable dances were the can-can, the quadrille and the chahut.

♦ THE MOULIN ROUGE
One of the most
famous multi-purpose
night-spots in Paris
was the Moulin Rouge
on the boulevard de
Clichy (here in a late
nineteenth-century
photograph). More
luxurious than the
Moulin de la Galette,
it was opened in 1889.

♦ SEURAT'S CIRCUS
An acrobatic dancer
at the Fernando
Circus in Paris was
the subject of Seurat's
last, unfinished work,
The Circus, 1890-91
(Musée d'Orsay,
Paris).

CHA-U-KAO ♦
One of the most
famous attractions at
the Moulin Rouge was
Cha-U-Kao, a
female clown, often
painted by Toulouse-
Lautrec.

♦ POSTERS
A relatively new art
form, posters became
more widely used
thanks to booming
business and the
multi-print technique
of lithography.
Toulouse-Lautrec was
one of the first artists
to specialize in this
type of art. Above: a
poster of his from
1891 (Victoria and
Albert Museum,
London).

♦ BEHIND THE SCENES
Zidler was the most
famous director of
the Moulin Rouge at
the time. He
commissioned the
best artists, including
Toulouse-Lautrec, to
design the posters
advertising his shows.

ARTISTS OF THE PETIT BOULEVARD

While in Paris van Gogh did not mix with the most famous Impressionists, whom he called "of the Grand Boulevard". Rather, he painted, talked and exhibited his work with a smaller group of young artists whom he described as "of the Petit Boulevard" – Bernard, Toulouse-Lautrec and Anquetin. Meanwhile, there were many disputes in the Paris art world, particularly between Bernard and the group led by Seurat and Signac, who were accused of being excessively technical, scientific and cold. Van Gogh wanted to form a harmonious and unified community of artists, modeled on medieval brotherhoods and close to the people. He tried to organize exhibitions in his local cafés and bistros, to suit the tastes of ordinary men and women. There was a short happy period of sharing ideas, but soon all the members of the group went their separate ways.

♦ **AN EXHIBITION AT THE TAMBOURIN**
The young artists of the "Petit Boulevard" were able to exhibit their works when their friends kindly offered their cafés or restaurants as venues. Agostina Segatori allowed van Gogh to exhibit Japanese prints at her café, the Tambourin, during the spring of 1887. She was probably the model for his painting of *The Italian Woman* (left), December 1887 (Musée d'Orsay, Paris).

♦ **HENRI DE TOULOUSE-LAUTREC**
Henri de Toulouse-Lautrec (1864-1901) was left with stunted legs after two falls during his teens. Later, he became the archetypal isolated and rebellious artist and is best known for his clear-eyed pictures of Paris nightlife, including the dancers at the Moulin Rouge; but he had not yet gained this reputation when he was part of the "Petit Boulevard" group and friendly with van Gogh. Two of his works from this period are reproduced here. Far left: *Carmen*, 1884 (Sterling and Francine Clark Art Institute, Williamstown, Massachusetts). Left: *Portrait of the Countess de Toulouse-Lautrec in the salon of the château at Malromé*, 1886-87 (Musée Lautrec, Albi).

10. VAN GOGH'S LIFE ♦ *Young artists in Montmartre would meet at Père Tanguy's, look at paintings and discuss ideas heatedly. It was here that van Gogh often saw Paul Gauguin. But he could not stand all the disputes and would often leave without having said a word. He wrote to Bernard: "If we really believe that Signac and the other 'pointillists' often do good work, then instead of tearing their paintings to pieces we should give them recognition and talk about them respectfully. Otherwise we become narrow-minded sectarians." At the same time, it was in his own nature to create difficult situations. Theo wrote to their sister that life with Vincent was "intolerable", but eventually matters improved. Van Gogh organized some small exhibitions of the "Petit Boulevard" in some of the Montmartre cafés.* ⇒+

♦ **LOUIS ANQUETIN**
Louis Anquetin (1861-1932) was another member of the "Petit Boulevard" group. He pioneered cloisonnism with Bernard, to whom he dedicated his *Portrait of Emile Bernard*, c.1887 (Rijksmuseum Vincent van Gogh, Amsterdam).

♦ **EMILE BERNARD**
Emile Bernard (1868-1941) was one of the brightest intellects in the Paris art world. He turned away from Impressionism and divisionism, using symbolism and creating an atmosphere of mystery in which people and things took on a spiritual meaning. He also adopted a new technique, cloisonnism, in which areas of bright, flat color were enclosed by dark outlines. Far left: clearly outlined, simplified forms and intense colors, in a detail from *Breton Women in the Fields*, 1888 (Private collection). Left: *Self-portrait, to my Friend Vincent*, 1888 (Rijksmuseum Vincent van Gogh, Amsterdam).

♦ **A QUARREL AT A SHOW**
In November 1887 van Gogh organized a "Petit Boulevard" exhibition at the Restaurant du Chalet in Montmartre, near the junction between the avenue Saint-Ouen and the avenue de Clichy. About a hundred paintings by van Gogh, Bernard, Toulouse-Lautrec, Anquetin and perhaps even Gauguin were hung on the restaurant walls. Bernard sold his first painting there, and van Gogh was very proud of the occasion. Later, however, things took a turn for the worse. As Bernard reported, "this left-wing exhibition of our incendiary works came to a miserable end. A violent quarrel broke out between Vincent and the restaurant owner. Vincent then got hold of a wheelbarrow and moved the whole exhibition to his studio in the rue Lepic."

SELF-PORTRAIT IN FRONT OF THE EASEL

This work was painted at a critical time in van Gogh's life and in his development as an artist, at the end of his stay in Paris. In the grip of depression, he looked for answers to many questions about himself. Painting a self-portrait was a way of delving deep into his own personality.

♦ THE LOOK
More than showing how van Gogh's appearance altered over time, his self-portraits are evidence of his volatile character. He was given to outbursts of anger, yet capable of great tenderness. Above: *Self-portrait*, 1887 (Rijksmuseum Kröller-Müller, Otterlo).

♦ THE WORK
Self-portrait in front of the Easel, 1888, oil on canvas, 65.5 x 50.5 cm (26 x 20 in) (Rijksmuseum Vincent van Gogh, Amsterdam). Dated January 1888, this was one of the last works van Gogh painted in Paris. At this time he was going through a period of deep depression. Painting did not always help him overcome the attacks, but more and more often, during his last months in the city, he would shut himself in his studio and examine his face in the mirror, to produce a self-portrait. He painted about ten in this way and explained in a letter to his sister Wilhelmina: "My intention is to show that a variety of very different portraits can be made of the same person." The letter also contains information about the colors he used: "A basic palette of lemon yellow, vermilion, malachite green and cobalt blue. Just all the basic palette colors, except the orange for the beard. The figure is set against a grey-blue background."

Because it was difficult and, at times, impossible to find models, van Gogh often used himself as the subject for his paintings. The self-portraits he produced were not as many in number as those painted by his fellow Dutch artist Rembrandt, but nonetheless they provide much evidence of his appearance and, above all, of his moods. There are forty-three moving and sometimes dramatic pictures of van Gogh, in all of which the eyes – often looking in two different directions – seem to be trying to make contact and communicate with the viewer.

♦ A DRAWING
Detail from a *Self-portrait*, 1887 (Rijksmuseum Vincent van Gogh, Amsterdam).

♦ THE DARK HAT
This dark-toned *Self-portrait* dates from 1886 or may even belong to the Nuenen period (Rijksmuseum Vincent van Gogh, Amsterdam).

♦ TWO YEARS EARLIER
Van Gogh painted this *Self-portrait in front of the Easel* in 1886 (Rijksmuseum Vincent van Gogh, Amsterdam). The dark colors are a sign that it belongs to the period van Gogh spent in Nuenen or Antwerp or to his early months in Paris.

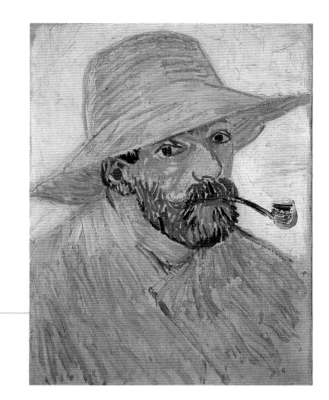

◆ THE LIGHT HAT
Self-portrait with Felt Hat, 1887-88 (Rijksmuseum Vincent van Gogh, Amsterdam). Now the colors are lighter and applied with Impressionist brush-strokes.

THE STRAW HAT ◆
Van Gogh looked unkempt and dressed carelessly. He loved hats and pipes, and both appear in this *Self-portrait*, painted in Arles in 1888 (Rijksmuseum Vincent van Gogh, Amsterdam).

LOST IN THOUGHT ◆
This *Self-portrait* (Musée d'Orsay, Paris) was painted in 1889 in the asylum at Saint-Rémy. Van Gogh looks "as pale as the devil", as he himself wrote to Theo.

◆ LIKENESS
A detail from *Self-portrait in front of the Easel*. Van Gogh wrote to his sister: "It is not easy to paint a self-portrait, at least when it has to be different from a photograph"; the aim was "to achieve a deeper resemblance than in a photograph".

◆ TOOLS OF THE TRADE
A detail from *Self-portrait in front of the Easel*. The brushes and palette are smeared with the pure colors van Gogh used in his painting: vermilion, blue, yellow and green.

HOW OTHERS ◆ PORTRAYED VAN GOGH
Many of van Gogh's friends, including Lautrec, Bernard and Gauguin, painted portraits of him. This one is by John Russell, 1886 (Rijksmuseum Vincent van Gogh, Amsterdam).

PAINTERS IN PROVENCE

The colors, atmosphere and scenery of Provence had attracted artists long before van Gogh. Several of the Impressionists spent some time in the South of France, notably Monet and Renoir, who eventually made his home there. Cézanne and Monticelli were Southerners who spent only a limited time in Paris before returning to their roots. One thing all the artists who came to Provence had in common was the importance that they placed on the study of color.

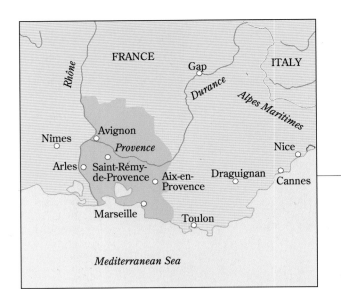

♦ **AN ANCIENT REGION**
Provence is a large, mountainous region in southern France. Its largest city is Marseille. To the east are the Alps, to the west, the river Rhône and to the south, the Mediterranean. It was an ancient Roman province. In the Middle Ages, the troubadours of Provence composed superb poetry and music.

VAN GOGH'S ♦ PROVENCE
In a letter to his sister, van Gogh explained: "Today my palette is filled with colors: sky blue, pink, orange, vermilion." Right: *Harvest on the Plain of La Crau*, 1888 (Rijksmuseum Vincent van Gogh, Amsterdam).

FRUIT TREES ♦
Fruit trees were one of the first subjects that van Gogh painted in Arles. The influence of Japanese art shows in *Pink Peach Tree in Blossom (Souvenir de Mauve)*, 1888 (Rijksmuseum Kröller-Müller, Otterlo).

♦**THE LANGLOIS BRIDGE**
Below: *The Langlois Bridge with Women Washing*, March 1888 (Rijksmuseum Kröller-Müller, Otterlo).
Van Gogh drew and painted many versions of the view of this bridge, which he discovered on his expeditions into the countryside around Arles. Aspects of this painting are reminiscent of Japanese prints of bridges.

♦ BRAQUE
With Pablo Picasso, Georges Braque (1882-1963) developed Cubism. He spent a short time in Provence in 1906-1907, attracted by the colors of the area and by its links with Cézanne, who was revered by many painters of Braque's generation.
Left: Braque, *Landscape at La Ciotat*, 1906 (Galerie Beyeler, Basel).

♦ SIGNAC
The divisionist painter Paul Signac (1863-1935) was one of the most regular visitors to the South of France. A friend of Seurat and van Gogh, he lived in Saint-Tropez for about twenty years.
Left: Signac, *Saint-Tropez – Storm*, 1895 (Musée de l'Annonciade, Saint-Tropez).

♦ CÉZANNE
Paul Cézanne (1839-1906) was born and died in Aix-en-Provence. He became an Impressionist for a time, but eventually created his own unique style, having a powerful influence on the development of modern art.
Above: Cézanne, *Mont Sainte-Victoire*, c.1887 (Courtauld Institute Galleries, London).

♦ GUIGOU
There had been an active school of local painters in Provence since the middle of the nineteenth century. Paul Guigou (1834-1871) painted *The Hills of Allauch near Marseille*, 1863 (Musée des Beaux-Arts, Marseille), in a straightforward Realist style.

♦ MATISSE
One of the greatest artists of modern times, Henri Matisse (1869-1954) was first struck by the colors of the South on the island of Corsica. He then spent several summers in Provence and later moved permanently to Nice.
Left: Matisse, *Collioure*, 1905 (Musée de l'Annonciade, Saint-Tropez).

11. VAN GOGH'S LIFE ♦ *In 1888, Vincent left Paris and went to live in Arles, in Provence. From there he wrote to his brother Theo: "I can hardly imagine coming back to work in Paris, unless there was a little place there to escape to, where one could recover and regain a sense of calm and some self-esteem. Without that, one would inevitably go mad." He set to work immediately in Arles and regularly sent his canvases to Theo, who was supporting him by sending him 250 francs a month. On May 1, he rented a wing of a building called the Yellow House with the intention of starting an artists' colony like the one at Pont-Aven in Brittany where his friend Paul Gauguin was staying.* ➢

VAN GOGH'S TECHNIQUE

As he studied painting, van Gogh experimented with all the styles and techniques of his time. His first models were Realist works in the style of Millet and the dark-colored paintings of his native Holland. Then he practised using the brighter colors of the Impressionists, trying to discover how to capture on the canvas the light and atmosphere of a particular moment. Studying divisionism represented an attempt to adopt a more scientific approach to his painting. Finally, he absorbed all of these influences, using whichever approach seemed suitable and developing a style of his own, characterized by strength and speedy execution. He was always ready to try new ideas, from squeezing paint directly out of the tube on to the canvas to painting night scenes, working in the open air by candlelight.

♦ **REFLECTIONS**
Vincent van Gogh, *Starry Night on the Rhône*, 1888 (Musée d'Orsay, Paris).

♦ **SUNFLOWERS**
In 1888, Paul Gauguin painted this *Portrait of Van Gogh Painting Sunflowers* (Rijksmuseum Vincent van Gogh, Amsterdam). Vincent said: "It's me – but me gone mad." Later, at a café, he suddenly threw a glass at Gauguin, who forced him back home and put him to bed. It was the first open sign of the tension between the two artists.

♦ **BALLS OF WOOL**
Van Gogh used the various-colored balls of wool in this Japanese box to study the effects of combinations of color.

PAINTS ♦
Van Gogh used tubes of oil paint, which had been manufactured industrially since 1846. They were easily obtainable and portable, making it possible to work out of doors. They completely replaced the paints that earlier artists had had to prepare themselves.

2   3

♦ **DARK TO LIGHT**
Van Gogh was always looking for a method that would allow him to represent light. At first, he studied and copied the techniques used by earlier artists. Then he discovered that light could be represented more effectively by using its prismatic constituents: that is, pure colors. The examples above show his developing ideas. 1. *Still Life with Bottles*, 1884-85 (Rijksmuseum Kröller-Müller, Otterlo); 2. *Still Life with Lemons*, detail, 1887 (Rijksmuseum Vincent van Gogh, Amsterdam); 3. *Still Life with Drawing Board*, 1889 (Rijksmuseum Kröller-Müller, Otterlo).

♦ **THE EASEL**
For painting out of doors, van Gogh always set up his easel. He devised a system of weighting it down so that it could not be blown over by the wind.

♦ **BY CANDLELIGHT**
Van Gogh's later technique enabled him to work very quickly, putting the main elements of the picture on to the canvas during a single session. To keep the freshness of his response, he tried to work directly from the subjects he portrayed, be they people, objects or landscapes. He thought up ingenious ways to achieve this, such as painting *Starry Night on the Rhône* with lighted candles attached to his straw hat and on his easel.

THE YELLOW HOUSE

This is a painting of the house that van Gogh rented in Arles, with the intention of turning it into a place where fellow artists could live in a kind of brotherhood, like a medieval guild. The Yellow House stood on the corner of a block of buildings near the station. In one direction, the rue Montmajour led under the railway and out of the city. In the other was the place Lamartine, a three-sided open area. In van Gogh's painting, heaps of earth can be seen on the road and in the area in front of the house.

♦ THE WORK
The Yellow House, 1888, oil on canvas, 72 x 91.5 cm (28 x 36 in) (Rijksmuseum Vincent van Gogh, Amsterdam). Van Gogh painted this work in September 1888, when he had been at Arles for seven months. Having rented the house in May, he had written immediately to Theo: "I enclose a quick sketch on wrapping paper, a grassy area on the [place Lamartine] where you come in to the city, with a house in the background. Well, today I rented the right wing of this house, which has four rooms, or rather two, with two boxrooms. The external walls are painted yellow and inside it is whitewashed, and it gets the sun all day; ... so now I can tell you about my idea to ask Bernard and others to send me their paintings ... at last I will be able to see my paintings in a well-lit environment."

♦ PLACE LAMARTINE
A drawing by van Gogh of the area in front of the house, 1888 (Rijksmuseum Vincent van Gogh, Amsterdam).

♦ A FIGURE
The man walking along the footpath in front of the house appears in both the oil painting (above) and the watercolor (below).

The colors of Provence soon made their mark on van Gogh's palette: yellow and blue became the colors that he used the most. He used a perspective method that he had already employed in the past: he arranged his picture following a kind of grid of guidelines. The painting of The Yellow House *is built on two diagonals: one on the right gives the effect of depth, tapering off under the railway bridge; the other is the line of the edge of the square. The heaps of earth in the foreground give a sense of distance between the viewer and the house. But the contrasting colors are what count in this painting. "The vault of the sky ... is a magnificent blue; the rays of the sun are a pale sulphur yellow, and this combination of colors is delicate and pleasing."*

♦ A WATERCOLOR
As well as the oil painting, van Gogh painted this watercolor of *The Yellow House* in September-October 1888 (Rijksmuseum Vincent van Gogh, Amsterdam).

♦ **DETAILS**
Left: details from *The Yellow House*. The blue of the sky (top) has been created using thick, oily, intensely colored paint spread with a palette knife. In the yellow light reflected from the walls of the building, daily life goes on peacefully. As well as the customers sitting outside the café (center), there are people out walking, a mother with her children, and a train (bottom), puffing clouds of smoke, crossing the railway bridge.

♦ **AROUND ARLES**
Van Gogh arrived in Provence in the middle of winter and found that it was snowing. However, he was still struck by the colors and the light. He could never stop exploring the area. Ignoring the Roman ruins, he went to the banks of the Rhône and to the coast. At the end of June 1888, he painted *Fishing Boats on the Beach at Saintes-Maries* (Rijksmuseum Vincent van Gogh, Amsterdam).

♦ **THE HIGH YELLOW NOTE**
Yellow – "the high yellow note" that van Gogh said he had found – became one of the colors he used most frequently while he was at Arles.
It is the main color in all the many versions of *Sunflowers* (top: 1889, Rijksmuseum Vincent van Gogh, Amsterdam); and of the above painting of *Haystacks in Provence*, 1888 (Rijksmuseum Kröller-Müller, Otterlo).

PEOPLE OF ARLES

At the end of the nineteenth century, there was a great difference between a capital city with millions of inhabitants and a quiet provincial town.

Physically, Arles was a long train journey away from Paris; but in their lifestyles the two places were even further apart. In Arles, life was based on the principles and values of country life. Van Gogh much preferred the sincerity of the people of Arles to the confusion of Paris. Everyone in the cafés in the evenings knew everyone else, and the skies and colors of Provence were all around to be enjoyed.

♦ THE ROULINS
In mid-August 1888, van Gogh got to know the postal worker Joseph Roulin and his family. He painted many portraits of them while he was in Arles.
Left: *Joseph Roulin*, 1889 (Museum of Fine Arts, Boston).
Left below: *La Berceuse*, 1889 (Private collection). This is a portrait of Joseph's wife holding the cord with which she can rock the baby's cradle.

♦ CAFÉ ALCAZAR
The Yellow House in Arles was destroyed during the Second World War, but the nearby Café Alcazar (above), at number 2 place Lamartine, is still standing today. The café was the subject of one of van Gogh's paintings, which he described in a letter to Theo: "In *The Night Café* I have tried to convey that a café is a place where you can ruin yourself, go mad, commit a crime .... So I have tried to express, as it were, the powers of darkness in a low public house."

IN THE CAFÉ ♦
The café was one of the few meeting-places to go to at the end of a hard day – which, for most people in Arles, meant working in the fields. It was somewhere to drink a glass of wine, eat a hot meal prepared in a back room, and doze off on the table.

12. VAN GOGH'S LIFE ♦ *From Arles, Vincent wrote to Theo: "I am seeing a lot of new things here, I am learning, and my body, if treated with a little kindness, serves me well." He made friends with the Ginoux family and the postal worker Roulin. All the time he painted and, at the end of July, he sent his brother 35 pictures. He kept inviting Paul Gauguin to stay with him and finally, thanks to Theo's intervention and promise to help financially, Gauguin agreed. Van Gogh was excited by his arrival at the Yellow House, but their relationship soon deteriorated. They were opposite personalities: van Gogh tormented, impetuous and untidy, Gauguin apparently self-confident and meticulous. Gauguin found Arles boring and the fear that he might leave put a strain on Vincent. ≫→*

BILLIARDS ♦
Unlike the fashionable cafés in Paris, taverns in the sleepy French provinces rarely provided attractions or entertainment. A billiard table and playing cards were all that a café like the Alcazar could offer its customers.

♦ L'ARLÉSIENNE
Both Gauguin and van Gogh painted Marie Ginoux, wife of the hotel-keeper Joseph Ginoux. With her Mediterranean features and wearing the local dress, she represented a typical woman from Arles. Left: van Gogh, *L'Arlésienne*, 1890 (Museu de Arte, São Paulo, Brazil).

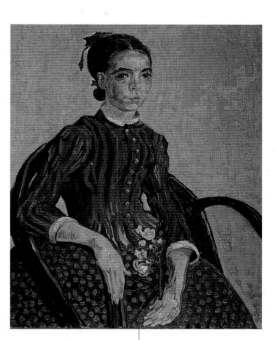

♦ LA MOUSMÉ
This portrait of 1888 (National Gallery of Art, Washington) is of a young woman from Arles, but van Gogh took the title *La Mousmé* (an attendant in a Japanese teahouse) from Pierre Loti's novel *Madame Chrysanthème*, which he had just read.

♦ JOSEPH ROULIN
Van Gogh described Roulin the postal worker as a man "with a great beard, very similar to Socrates", a cheerful old radical who proved to be his only true friend in Arles.

BEDROOM IN ARLES

Van Gogh described this painting of his bedroom in the Yellow House, in a letter of 1888: "It is just simply my bedroom .... The walls are pale violet. The floor is covered with red tiles, the wooden bedhead and chairs are as yellow as fresh butter, the sheets and pillows are very pale lemon green. The blanket is scarlet. The window green. The wash-stand is orange and the basin blue. The doors are lilac .... There are some paintings on the wall, a towel and some clothes."

♦ **THE WORK**
Bedroom in Arles, 1888, oil on canvas, 72 x 90 cm (28 x 35 in) (Rijksmuseum Vincent van Gogh, Amsterdam). The work was painted in October 1888, as we know from a letter bearing that date which van Gogh wrote to Gauguin: "I have painted ... my bedroom, with its ... wood furniture as you know. Well, I really enjoyed doing this stark interior with Seurat-style simplicity. The colors are uniform but applied roughly, without thinning the paint .... I wanted all these different colors to express a totally restful feeling. There is just one dash of white, in the black-framed mirror .... You will see the painting with the others and we can talk about it, because I often don't know what I am doing, since I am working as if I were a sleep-walker." There are two other versions of the painting, both in oils and produced in September 1889. One is at the Musée d'Orsay, Paris, and the other at the Art Institute, Chicago. Above and below are two details from the 1888 version.

♦ **A DRAWING FOR THEO**
Vincent described the painting in a letter to Theo in October 1888.

He enclosed the above drawing of it (Rijksmuseum Vincent van Gogh, Amsterdam).

Van Gogh believed that his painting of his bedroom in the Yellow House was a real achievement: he had found a style of his own and a technique of which he felt confident. He produced two replicas of the painting a year later. The technique used in the painting had gone beyond divisionism and Impressionism. The colors were uniform; a palette knife had created broad, flat surfaces; the complementary colors gave an effect of both harmony and energy. Van Gogh had reached a point where his style displayed a considerable degree of freedom. This included freedom from rules of perspective, shown in the arbitrary way in which the surfaces of the table and chair are arranged against the background.

♦ **OUTLINES**
A detail from *Bedroom in Arles*. Van Gogh was now constructing his compositions using color – intended both to communicate feelings and to create harmony. However, he still used dark outlines.

◆ PERSPECTIVE
In Arles, van Gogh painted some works, like *Bedroom in Arles*, in which the perspective was more or less correct, and others where he treated perspective more freely.

◆ JUXTAPOSING COLORS
This detail from *Bedroom in Arles* shows how van Gogh deliberately paired complementary colors. Here, yellow is placed next to violet, blue with orange, red with green. As Chevreul had pointed out, the effect of juxtaposing complementary colors is that each intensifies the impact of the other. Van Gogh wanted the overall effect of harmony to convey the feeling of "rest", to give a reassuring image of his own daily life.

◆ PAINTINGS ON THE WALLS
A detail from *Bedroom in Arles*. Van Gogh's room is shown as simple and tidy and equipped with everyday, basic objects. The paintings on the walls include two portraits (above) and a landscape.

◆ TWO CHAIRS
In December 1888, van Gogh produced two paintings of chairs: left, *Gauguin's Chair* (Rijksmuseum Vincent van Gogh, Amsterdam) and, right, *Chair with Pipe* (National Gallery, London), which represents his own chair. The difference between the two is a sign of van Gogh's high regard for Gauguin, whose portrait he never dared paint. Gauguin's chair is more ornate than van Gogh's. The books in the picture allude to his being a man of culture and the candle is lit (unlike van Gogh's pipe).

GAUGUIN

Like van Gogh, Paul Gauguin was an artist for long misunderstood, who suffered and struggled as he developed his ideas and became a great innovator. He broke away from Impressionism to work in a new style, Synthetism, which he and Emile Bernard developed together. Because of his strong personality and mature age, he became an influence on many young painters.

♦ VASE WITH BRETON SCENES
Ceramic, 29 cm (11½ in) high, 1887-88 (Musée Royaux d'Art et d'Histoire, Brussels).

♦ HIS LIFE
Paul Gauguin was born in Paris in 1848, but spent his childhood in Lima, Peru, as well as in the French cities of Rouen and Orléans. He joined the merchant marines, traveling around the world, and then worked as a stockbroker in Paris. Meanwhile Pissarro was encouraging him to paint, and he began to adopt the style and techniques of the Impressionists. When he lost his job in 1883, he decided to devote himself entirely to painting. This was the start of a troubled life marked by a need to escape and explore. He left his wife and children and moved to Brittany, then to Panama and Martinique, then back to Pont-Aven in Brittany, to Arles to stay with van Gogh, to Brittany again, and finally to Tahiti and the Marquesas Islands. In Polynesia he hoped that he had finally found the paradise on earth that he had sought: a simple, untainted and primitive place. In all the tumult of his artistic activity, Gauguin found time not only for painting but also for sculpture, ceramics and writing. He died in 1903 in the Marquesas Islands.

♦ A SELF-PORTRAIT VASE
1889 (Kunstindustrimuseet, Copenhagen). Gauguin began to produce ceramics in 1886. Often, as in this example, he took his inspiration from Inca terracotta work seen in his childhood in Peru.

♦ TO HIS FRIEND VINCENT
Shortly before going to stay with Vincent van Gogh in Arles, Gauguin painted this *Self-portrait (Les Misérables)*, 1888 (Rijksmuseum Vincent van Gogh, Amsterdam). He wrote about the painting in a letter, remarking that the artist looks like "a powerful and roughly-dressed bandit".

♦ THE FIRST TAHITIAN PORTRAIT
Vahine no te Tiare (Woman with Flower), 1891 (Ny Carlsberg Glyptotek, Copenhagen), was the first portrait of a native woman that Gauguin painted in Polynesia. He must have been annoyed to find that the girl insisted on being painted in her Sunday best dress. Later he made most of his models wear the pre-colonial *pareo* (wraparound skirt).

THE SAVAGE ♦
Oviri, 1894 (Musée d'Orsay, Paris). Gauguin produced this ceramic in Paris, after his first trip to Polynesia. The title *Oviri* means "savage" – an adjective that Gauguin liked to apply to himself. In Polynesia, he found the primitive dimension he had been searching for during his stays in Brittany. The primitive art of Africa and Oceania would later inspire artists like Picasso.

♦ **PARADISE ON EARTH**
Gauguin arrived in Tahiti for the first time in June 1891, after a sea voyage lasting almost three months. He had raised the money for the trip by auctioning his paintings.
Left: *Nevermore*, 1894 (Courtauld Institute Galleries, London). When he painted this, Gauguin had committed himself to spend the rest of his life in Polynesia. It conveys the sense of mystery that he found in these enchanting islands.

♦ **THE PONT-AVEN SCHOOL**
Clear outlines, large areas of juxtaposed complementary colors, no shading, no attempt to convey a sense of depth, and a very free representation of reality: these were the principles that inspired a group of painters who gathered in the Breton village of Pont-Aven. Their leader from 1888 was Gauguin, but other important members were Paul Sérusier and Maxime Maufra. Above: a detail from Sérusier's *The Talisman*, 1888 (Musée d'Orsay, Paris). Above right: Maufra, *Landscape at Pont-Aven*, 1890 (Musée des Beaux-Arts, Quimper).

SYNTHETISM ♦
The sacred, the primitive and the mysterious had already appeared in Gauguin's paintings during his Breton period. *Jacob's Struggle with the Angel* (right), 1888 (National Gallery of Scotland, Edinburgh), is an example. Gauguin broke away from naturalism to develop a simplified style that would convey the essence of things (Synthetism). He recommended painting from memory, rather than from objects in front of the artist. In this he differed from van Gogh, whose works were usually painted from reality.

STARRY NIGHT

In painting this scene, van Gogh was probably combining real and imaginary, Provençal and northern elements, and so it has been suggested that he was remembering Holland in the village on the right. But, there have been various interpretations of *Starry Night*. It may be a representation, in van Gogh's most visionary style, of the sky in June 1889, expressing emotions inexpressible in any other medium; but another suggestion is that the galactic turbulence is a symbol for Christ's Passion.

♦ **THE CHURCH TOWER**
A detail from *Starry Night*. The sleeping village with its little church plays a distinctly secondary role compared with the spectacle of the starry sky.

♦ **THE WORK**
Starry Night, 1889, oil on canvas, 73.7 x 92.1 cm (29 x 36 in) (Museum of Modern Art, New York). Van Gogh worked on this painting in June 1889, at the mental hospital in Saint-Rémy to which he had admitted himself the previous month. At this time, he was particularly interested in cypress trees, writing: "I constantly think about cypresses. I would like to do something with them as I did with the pictures of sunflowers, for I am amazed that they have not been done in the way I see them. The line and proportions of a cypress resemble those of an Egyptian obelisk." The hospital allowed van Gogh to go out during the day with his canvases, easel and paints. The subjects he found to paint were dry-stone walls, hills, villages, olive trees and cypresses. The village in *Starry Night* could be Saint-Rémy, with some changes made, especially to the church tower, to give it a northern feel.

♦ **STUDIES OF THE SWIRLS**
The above drawing dated 1889 (Kunsthalle, Bremen) shows how carefully van Gogh studied – line by line – each individual swirl that makes up the image. Often painstaking preparatory work is done to produce a painting that looks spontaneous.

♦ **THE STARS**
A detail from *Starry Night*. A few yellow and white brush-strokes on a blue background make the stars burst open like flares.

While he was in the hospital at Saint-Rémy, van Gogh alternated between periods of hyperactivity and long spells of deep depression. His altered state of mind was reflected in a change in his style of painting. During the time he spent in Arles, his work had been characterized by the use of pure colors, uniformly spread in large areas. At Saint-Rémy, however, grey, ochre and blended colors made their appearance again. These were much the same colors as he had used for his paintings in Nuenen, but he used lighter tones of them now. Another change was that the energy previously expressed in color made itself felt, instead, in the lines in the painting. They twisted and turned, writhed, flared and became grouped in great swirls, filling the canvas with movement. The result was a dynamic style of painting in which the artist's inner turmoil was projected on to the world.

♦ **VAN GOGH'S SYMBOLISM**
A detail from *Starry Night*. Some critics have suggested that van Gogh meant to do more than represent the world in a naturalistic way and that he included certain elements in his paintings as symbols, to communicate a more complex message. Seen from this point of view, the cypress tree in the left-hand foreground of *Starry Night*, linking the earth with the sky, could be understood as a symbol of death.

♦ NOCTURNAL SCENES
For some time van Gogh had been trying to show that the night, like the day, is full of colors that artists should capture rather than painting with the usual blacks.
Left: *Café Terrace at Night*, complete and detail, 1888 (Rijksmuseum Kröller-Müller, Otterlo).
Below: *Starry Night on the Rhône*, detail, 1888 (Musée d'Orsay, Paris).

♦ THE MOVING LINE
A new style emerged in van Gogh's painting after the period in Arles and while he was in hospital at Saint-Rémy. It can be seen in *Starry Night* and in other paintings of this time. Instead of the large, luminous areas of pure color that characterized his earlier paintings, van Gogh now used long brush-strokes to create undulating movement across the whole canvas. Both *The Alpilles with Olive Trees*, above (Private collection), and *Cypresses*, right (Metropolitan Museum of Art, New York), were painted in Saint-Rémy in June 1889.

THE ASYLUM

Nineteenth-century lunatic asylums (or, as they are now more often called, mental hospitals) varied in the treatment they offered. Patients might find themselves forcibly restrained, or in the care of enthusiastic experimenters, or even in the hands of eccentric charlatans. For a long time, most asylums had born a close resemblance to prisons. Mental illness was only ever handled humanely if the patient had some social status or if he or she was fortunate enough to find a sympathetic doctor. However, towards the end of the century, a new, scientific approach to mental disorders was taking form. In 1885, a young Viennese doctor, Sigmund Freud, went to meet the famous neurologist Jean-Martin Charcot at the Salpêtrière hospital in Paris. Charcot's influence was important in Freud's evolution into the father of psychoanalysis and in the beginning of the new approach to mental illness. In 1889, van Gogh admitted himself to the asylum at Saint-Rémy in Provence. The living conditions he found there were better than average for the time.

♦ **DR REY**
Van Gogh was fortunate to meet understanding doctors like Dr Félix Rey, who worked at the Arles hospital. Later, his life at the Saint-Rémy asylum was quiet and calm. Theo paid for Vincent's room and board at this private institution. Patients were left to their own devices, the only treatment being hydrotherapeutic bathing.
Left: Van Gogh, *Portrait of Dr Rey*, 1889 (Pushkin Museum, Moscow).

♦ **AT ARLES**
At the hospital in Arles, when he was not resting or talking with Dr Rey, van Gogh drew and painted other patients and the hospital itself.
Left: *Courtyard of the Arles Hospital*, April 1889 (Oskar Reinhart Collection, Winterthur).

♦ **FREUD**
A young Viennese doctor, Sigmund Freud, the future father of psychoanalysis, was present at Professor Charcot's lectures.

13. VAN GOGH'S LIFE ♦ *It became clear that van Gogh and Gauguin could not live together. They had many arguments and, according to Gauguin, on December 23, 1888, Vincent followed his friend into the street and threatened him with a razor. On the same night, he cut off his own earlobe, wrapped it in newspaper and took it to Rachel, a prostitute in a nearby brothel. Next morning the police found him unconscious in his bed at the Yellow House. He was taken to the Arles hospital, but his recovery was short-lived and the local people turned against him. On May 8, 1889, van Gogh admitted himself to the Saint-Paul-de-Mausole asylum, near Saint-Rémy. Here Dr Peyron diagnosed epilepsy and van Gogh seemed to be improving. He could paint, draw and talk to the other patients. Then, in July, he had another serious attack, during which he swallowed some paint.* ⇒

♦ THE CUT EAR
Van Gogh cut off his own earlobe after an argument with Gauguin in the Yellow House on December 23, 1888. Despite this complete breakdown, van Gogh seemed to recover quickly. Left: *A Self-portrait* of January 1889 (Courtauld Institute Galleries, London) shows how van Gogh saw himself at this time, with his ear bandaged.

♦ STRAITJACKETS
In the nineteenth century and long after, a mentally ill person was often strapped into a straitjacket.

♦ CHARCOT AT THE SALPÊTRIÈRE
Professor Jean-Martin Charcot gave his lectures on hypnosis as a treatment for hysteria, at the Salpêtrière. This prestigious university building had formerly been an asylum for mentally ill women. Humane methods of treatment had first been tried out there during the French Revolution.

♦ TREATING THE MENTALLY ILL
Dr Rey was not a specialist but had the good sense to advise van Gogh not to drink. On the other hand, Dr Théophile Peyron, the director of the hospital at Saint-Rémy, was more lax in his treatment. For example, he did not forbid alcohol; in fact, van Gogh described his system sarcastically: "It must be easy to treat the sick here: absolutely nothing is done for them."
Before Freud and the development of psychoanalysis, methods of treating the insane and studies of the mind and its neuroses were very rudimentary. There was a fashionable belief in the importance of measurable physiological factors. Insanity and criminal tendencies were thought to reveal themselves in certain aspects of a person's physical appearance. It was believed that by measuring the capacity of the cranium and by interpreting physical attributes, it was possible to control, predict and combat crime. However, Jean-Martin Charcot (1825-1893) laid the foundations for modern neuropathology during this period. He lectured in Paris, at the Sorbonne and, from 1882, at the Salpêtrière. A photograph of him is shown at the top of this column.

DOCTOR GACHET

Doctor Paul Gachet, a friend of artists and an artist himself, took care of van Gogh during the period when he was living in the town of Auvers. In one of his letters, van Gogh described how he was painting the doctor: "I am working on his portrait, he is wearing a white cap, he is very blond, very fair, even the skin on his hands is pinkish, a blue suit and a cobalt blue background; he is leaning on a red table."

♦ **IN AND AROUND AUVERS**
At Auvers, van Gogh experienced a short, peaceful period of working calmly. The town, its surroundings and its inhabitants all became part of the world of his paintings.
Left: *Dr Gachet's Garden in Auvers*, May 1890 (Musée d'Orsay, Paris).

♦ **DR GACHET IN 1890**
This photograph shows Paul Gachet at the age of sixty-two, at the time when he and van Gogh were friends.

♦ **THE WORK**
Portrait of Dr Gachet, June 1890, oil on canvas, 68 x 57 cm (27 x 22½ in) (Musée d'Orsay, Paris). Van Gogh painted this portrait, and several others of the doctor and members of his family, on one of the many occasions that he visited Gachet during May and June 1890. "Nothing, absolutely nothing could keep me here except Gachet," he wrote to his brother Theo. "I always feel that I can work quite easily in his house, every time I go there, and he always asks me to lunch either on Sundays or Mondays." Paul-Ferdinand Gachet (1828-1909) had studied medicine in Paris but, while he was still a student, he had become interested in art and had been in contact with Gustave Courbet and his followers.
After he moved to Auvers, outside the capital, he still kept a clinic open in Paris. He was a socialist and a Darwinian, and became a defender of modern artists, especially Cézanne and Pissarro. An artist himself and good at drawing, he introduced van Gogh to etching.

♦ **PORTRAITS, NOT PHOTOGRAPHS**
Van Gogh created three portraits of his friend Paul Gachet.
Above: *Portrait of Gachet with Pipe*, etching, May 1890 (Rijksmuseum Kröller-Müller, Otterlo).
The artist described his plans for these pictures: "I would like to make these portraits so that they seem like living presences to people who see them in a hundred years from now. I am trying to achieve this, not by producing photographic likenesses, but by empathetic expression" – that is, by trying to feel what the person is feeling, in order to express his or her soul, or essence, in the painting.

♦ **ANOTHER VERSION**
In June 1890 van Gogh painted this second version in oils of the portrait of Gachet (Private collection). Here we can see traces of the artist's Saint-Rémy style, with swarms of small brush-strokes following the contours.

While he was in Auvers, van Gogh seems to have tried to keep his imagination under control. The twisting, swirling, emphatic lines of the paintings he had produced in Saint-Rémy now disappeared from his work. They were replaced by an approach that was much calmer and more reflective, showing a new desire for order and tranquillity. The portrait of Gachet shows the doctor's melancholy nature. Van Gogh wrote that the face had "the heart-broken expression of our time".

♦THE EYES AND THE SOUL
A detail from *Portrait of Dr Gachet*. Van Gogh tried to get right inside his subject's mind, in order to be able to portray his inner being, or soul. He saw the doctor as a melancholy, thoughtful man, and wrote about him to his sister: "I have found a true friend in Gachet. He is something like a brother, we resemble each other physically and spiritually as well, he is also nervous and odd ... like you and me. He is older and has been a widower for a few years, but he is a doctor through and through, and his faith and vocation give him the strength to carry on."

THE FOXGLOVE ♦
In painting the stem of foxglove in Gachet's hand, van Gogh was making a deliberate reference to the doctor's profession. Gachet was a homoeopathic doctor who used plants in his medicines.

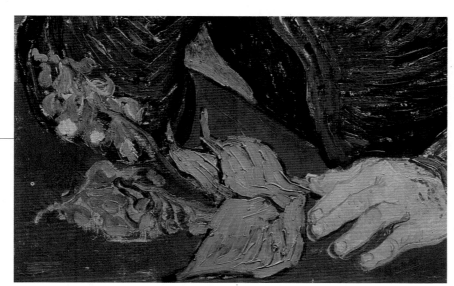

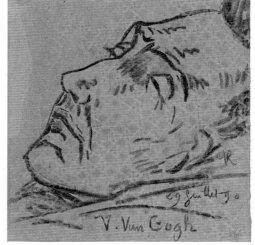

♦THE LAST PORTRAIT
This was the last portrait made of Vincent van Gogh. It was drawn as he lay on his deathbed, on July 29, 1890, by his friend and doctor, Paul Gachet (Musée d'Orsay, Paris).

♦DR GACHET AND CÉZANNE
In 1873, Dr Gachet had persuaded Paul Cézanne to come to Auvers. Several paintings and engravings by Cézanne date from the time he spent there.
Left: Cézanne, *Dr Gachet in the Studio*, 1873 (Musée d'Orsay, Paris).
Right: Cézanne, *Dr Gachet's House at Auvers*, 1873 (Musée d'Orsay, Paris).

THE ART MARKET

Today, van Gogh's paintings fetch the highest prices at auctions around the world, but in his lifetime he sold only one painting. Not everyone was so unlucky. Other painters did better and some of them became quite wealthy. Still, in late-nineteenth-century France, it was an uphill struggle for artists who did not paint in the style approved by dominant institutions such as the Salon and the academies. They spent their lives in temporary lodgings, often in poverty, finding it difficult to sell their work unless they found wealthy and enlightened patrons. Even in the twentieth century, it was from such humble studios, usually in the district of Montmartre, that painters like Picasso and Modigliani emerged.

♦**THE FIRST DEALERS** While conventional artists could count on public and private purchasers for their work, the innovative Impressionist painters had to rely on dealers, speculators and a few wealthy patrons with advanced tastes. This was the beginning of the modern free market in works of art. Many early buyers of Impressionist paintings were businessmen and professionals (including many doctors, like Gachet). There were a few professional dealers, such as Paul Durand-Ruel, but most were shopkeepers or restauranteurs who accepted paintings, instead of money, in payment of bills, and often had no clear idea of the value of the works that came into their possession in this way. Among such people were the confectioner Eugène Murer, the margarine manufacturer Auguste Pellerin, the mattress-maker Père Soulier, and also second-hand dealers, picture framers and sellers of artists' materials such as Père Tanguy. One pioneering dealer who recognized the value of the new artists was Ambroise Vollard, originally a notary. His photograph appears at the top of this column. For just a few francs, he bought the paintings that Theo van Gogh left behind at the Boussod and Valadon gallery. These included many works by Vincent and some by Gauguin.

♦**A MEAL AT A TAVERN** Above: van Gogh, *La Guinguette* (a tavern in Montmartre), 1886 (Rijksmuseum Vincent van Gogh, Amsterdam). During the 1880s, the average monthly wage of an office worker in Paris was 125 francs. A meal at a tavern in Montmartre cost 90 centimes. Painters sometimes paid with one of their canvases.

♦**VAN GOGH'S ONLY SALE** *The Red Vineyard*, painted at Arles in November 1888 (Pushkin Museum, Moscow), was the only painting that van Gogh sold during his lifetime.

14. VAN GOGH'S LIFE ♦ *In summer 1889, van Gogh had a serious mental collapse at Saint-Rémy, but his letters show that his intermittent attacks did not prevent him from expressing himself with exceptional lucidity and awareness, even about his own condition. Although for part of the time he was at his worst, medically speaking, at Saint-Rémy he produced 150 paintings and, as Emile Bernard wrote, "perhaps he had never painted so well". Meanwhile, Theo van Gogh had married Johanna Bonger, the sister of a friend, in Amsterdam in April 1889. He agreed that his brother should move to Auvers-sur-Oise, just outside Paris, where Dr Gachet could supervise him.* ➳

♦ RECORD AUCTIONS
Van Gogh wrote sadly about his own problems in trying to achieve any success in selling his work. The only painting he ever sold, *The Red Vineyard*, was bought by the sister of his friend, the poet Eugène Boch. And Theo van Gogh encountered great difficulties trying to get his brother's work appreciated and its value recognized. All these facts make it bitterly ironical that a painting by van Gogh has since become the most expensive work ever to be sold. The *Portrait of Dr Gachet* of 1890, once in the Metropolitan Museum of Art in New York, was sold at auction in that city on May 15, 1990, for $82,500,000. Three years before, van Gogh's *Irises*, 1889 (left, Paul Getty Museum, Malibu, California), had been sold for $53,900,000, also in New York.

THE AUCTIONEER ♦
At an auction, the auctioneer is responsible for knocking down (that is, selling) every lot. He bangs his gavel on his desk to indicate that the bidding is over.

THE NOTICE-BOARD ♦
Nowadays a notice-board displays updated information on the prices fetched by objects in the auction, with the equivalent amounts shown in the principal currencies.

♦ THE BUYER
Bidders raise their numbered signs to indicate their willingness to buy. The object on sale is knocked down to the last bidder to hold up his or her sign.

THE CHURCH AT AUVERS

Van Gogh described this painting in a letter to his sister Wilhelmina: "A large painting of the village church, executed so that the building appears purplish against a sky which is the deep and simple blue of pure cobalt; the windows seem stained with ultramarine; the roof is part violet, part orange. In front, there are flowers growing in the grass and some sunny, pink sand."

♦ **DETAILS**
Above and below: details of *The Church at Auvers*: the clock on the bell-tower and the tracery of a window.

♦ **THE WORK**
The Church at Auvers, June 1890, oil on canvas, 94 x 74 cm (37 x 29 in) (Musée d'Orsay, Paris). In the two months that he spent in Auvers, van Gogh produced about eighty paintings: more than one a day. He was active, he had stopped drinking and he had rediscovered the pleasure of painting outdoors. The subjects he chose were children, landscapes, portraits and the houses of the confectioner and of Daubigny (1817-1878), a painter of the Barbizon school who had lived in Auvers after leaving the Forest of Fontainebleau. By painting, van Gogh was trying to find a way out of the obsessions that had tormented him in recent months. The church of Notre-Dame is a twelfth- and thirteenth-century structure, built in a mixture of Romanesque and Gothic styles. Van Gogh's painting of it is one of his most highly-regarded and best-known works.

♦ **THE CHURCH TODAY**
The Romanesque-Gothic church of Notre-Dame, still the principal church in Auvers today.

♦ **THE TOWN HALL**
Van Gogh witnessed the life of Auvers. Above is a detail from *The Town Hall on 14 July*, 1890 (Private collection). The building had been decorated with flags for the anniversary of the storming of the Bastille – symbol of the beginning of the French Revolution.

♦ **DAUBIGNY'S GARDEN**
Below: Van Gogh, *The Garden of Daubigny's House*, 1890 (Öffentliche Kunstsammlung, Basel). Daubigny was an artist of the Barbizon school who lived in Auvers.

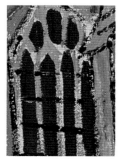

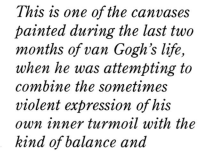

This is one of the canvases painted during the last two months of van Gogh's life, when he was attempting to combine the sometimes violent expression of his own inner turmoil with the kind of balance and integration normally characteristic of a finished work of art. As a result, the paintings are remarkably varied in mood and technique, swinging abruptly from agitation to serenity.

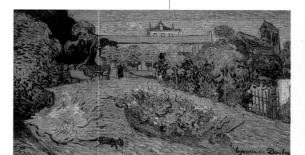

♦ LIGHT COLORS, FLOWING LINES
Left and right: details from *The Church at Auvers*. When van Gogh lived at Auvers, his palette became more colorful than ever. He still used strong contours, along with dynamic brush-strokes that flowed along them.

♦ FREEDOM FROM PERSPECTIVE
Left: a detail from *The Church at Auvers*. As you look at many works by van Gogh, it becomes clear that he has ignored the rules of linear perspective used to create a three-dimensional effect in the two-dimensional mediums of painting and drawing. For van Gogh, lines were not a means to imitate the kind of physical space seen in reality, but enabled him to impose his inner vision on the outside world.

WHEAT AND CROWS ♦
Van Gogh's troubled search for harmony at Auvers frequently gave way to tension and turbulence. It has often been suggested that there is a link between the agitated brush-strokes in *Wheatfield with Crows,* July 1890 (Rijks-museum Vincent van Gogh, Amsterdam), and the artist's imminent suicide, of which the black birds are seen as an omen.

♦ A CORNER OF AUVERS
Above: *Street and Steps in Auvers, with Figures*, late May 1890 (Saint Louis Art Museum, Saint Louis). In the two months that he spent at Auvers, van Gogh immersed himself in country life, producing paintings full of vitality, like the one shown here. They were brightly colored and often included human figures.

EXPRESSIONISM

Van Gogh did not have pupils or followers, and did not create a school of painting. He was a solitary genius, a loner, even though he could count on the esteem of a small number of fellow artists. Yet he made a fundamental contribution to the later development of modern art. The influence of his ideas and method of painting are most obvious in the works of the twentieth-century Expressionists, from the Fauves and the Die Brücke group to Edvard Munch.

♦ HENRI MATISSE
Matisse (1869-1954) was the leader of a group of artists whose work was characterized by their search for an emotional relationship with nature. In 1905 their first exhibition in Paris caused a scandal; they were named "Fauves" – wild beasts.
Left: *View of Collioure*, 1905 (Hermitage, St Petersburg).

♦ VAN GOGH'S EXPRESSIONISM
Van Gogh sought to convey the inner nature of things rather than merely representing the visible world. His expressive ability was noticed in 1890 by the critic, Albert Aurier: "His whole work is excessive: excess of strength, nervousness, expressive violence." The Expressionists took up this aspect of van Gogh's work.
Above: *Wheatfield with Crows*, detail, 1890 (Rijksmuseum Vincent van Gogh, Amsterdam).

♦ ANDRÉ DERAIN
One of the Fauves was the French painter, André Derain (1880-1954), a friend of Matisse and especially of Vlaminck. Later, he became a follower of Cézanne and a theoretician of Cubism. He moved away from the frenzy of pure color in his earlier work to more calm and reflective compositions which, especially after the First World War in which he fought as a soldier, showed the influence of the old masters such as the Italian Caravaggio (1571-1610).
Right: *Landscape at Collioure*, complete and detail, 1905 (National Gallery of Art, Washington). It is obvious from this painting that Derain's early style was influenced by the Expressionist outlook and, above all, by the paintings of van Gogh.

15. VAN GOGH'S LIFE ♦ *1890 started well. Theo sold one of his brother's paintings,* The Red Vineyard. *Vincent's move to Auvers in May and his friendship with Dr Gachet seemed to restore some calm to his life. In the next two months he produced about eighty paintings. In July, however, he was worried by Theo's financial difficulties. His letters reveal his bitter feelings about art dealers and a state of affairs in which a dead artist was valued more than a living one. On July 27, he went out to paint, and after he returned that evening, M et Mme Ravoux, with whom he lodged, discovered that he had shot himself with a revolver. Dr Gachet came at once and Theo was called to Vincent's bedside. Vincent died on July 29, after spending the day smoking his pipe and talking with his brother. Theo died on January 25, 1891, and was eventually buried next to Vincent in Auvers.*

♦ ERNST LUDWIG KIRCHNER
This German painter (1880-1938) was the driving force behind the group called Die Brücke, which he founded in 1905. These painters used color in a non-naturalistic way and distorted their subjects, to give their works a strong emotional impact. Left: *Woman in a Birch Wood*, 1906 (Thyssen Foundation, Madrid).

♦ MAURICE DE VLAMINCK

This French artist (1876-1958) began to paint in 1901, after seeing a van Gogh exhibition.

Left and right: *Houses and Trees*, complete and detail, 1906 (Metropolitan Museum of Art, New York). This shows Vlaminck's non-naturalistic, expressive use of pure color.

♦ ERICH HECKEL

Having studied architecture, Heckel (1883-1970) took up painting because of his fascination with the work of Edvard Munch and Vincent van Gogh. With Kirchner, in Dresden in 1905, he was one of the founders of the group known as Die Brücke. The work of these painters represented one extreme of German Expressionism. At the other extreme was the "spiritual" art of the Blaue Reiter group. Heckel's Expressionism is marked by a strong streak of aggression and, particularly just before the outbreak of the First World War, a feeling of anxiety. His style, like that of the other members of Die Brücke, is harsh, bold and full of emotional violence.

Left: Erich Heckel, *Brickwork*, 1907 (Thyssen Foundation, Madrid).

♦ EMIL NOLDE

Nolde (1867-1956) began work designing and carving furniture. Then, influenced by van Gogh, Gauguin and Munch, he turned to painting. For a time he was a member of the Die Brücke group, and took his inspiration from primitive art, old carvings and the colors in van Gogh's work.

Right: *In the Wheat*, 1906 (Nolde Foundation, Seebüll).

♦ EDVARD MUNCH

This Norwegian painter (1863-1944) traveled a great deal in France, Italy and Germany. He was influenced by the Impressionists, Gauguin and van Gogh. His own Expressionist style is based on the use of color to create unreal, anguished and highly dramatic scenes.

Right: *Starry Night*, 1924-25 (Munch Museet, Oslo).

◆ KEY DATES IN VAN GOGH'S LIFE

1853	Vincent Willem van Gogh was born on March 30 in the Dutch village of Groot Zundert. He was the eldest of six children of Theodorus, a Protestant minister, and Anna Cornelia Carbentus.
1857	His brother, Theo, was born on May 1. A close bond developed between the two brothers and greatly influenced both their lives.
1869	In August Vincent began work at The Hague branch of Goupil and Co., Paris art dealers.
1873	Theo was also employed by Goupil's, in the Brussels branch. In May, Vincent was transferred to London where he stayed for about two years.
1875	Vincent was moved to the Goupil head office in Paris, but he neglected his duties as he became more and more deeply religious.
1876	Having been dismissed on April 1, Vincent went to England as a teacher. In December, he returned to live with his parents who had moved to Etten.
1878	Wishing to become a lay preacher, Vincent enrolled in an evangelical training school near Brussels, but failed the course. At the end of the year, he went to the southern Belgian mining region of the Borinage, to preach and care for the poor and sick.
1880	Vincent moved to Brussels, where he met the Dutch painter Anton van Rappard. Theo was now sending him a little money.
1885	Vincent was living with his parents in Nuenen, where he produced many pictures of the peasant community, when his father died in March 1885. In November he moved to the Belgian city of Antwerp, where he enrolled in the Art Academy.
1886	Turned down for further study at the Antwerp Art Academy, Vincent went to Paris. He lived with Theo, who was now running the Boussod and Valadon gallery. At the Cormon atelier he met the artists Bernard, Toulouse-Lautrec and Anquetin.
1887	Vincent went often to Asnières, on the outskirts of Paris, where he and Bernard painted "en plein air" on the banks of the Seine.
1888	Vincent moved from Paris to Arles, in Provence, where he rented a wing of the Yellow House with the intention of setting up an artists' colony. He made friends with café owners Joseph and Marie Ginoux and with a postal worker, Joseph Roulin, and painted many portraits of them. In October, Paul Gauguin arrived to stay at the Yellow House. After an argument with him on December 23, Vincent cut off his own earlobe and took it to a prostitute he knew in a nearby brothel. The next morning he was found unconscious in his bed and was taken to the Arles hospital.
1889	On May 8, Vincent admitted himself to the Saint-Paul-de-Mausole asylum, near Saint-Rémy. In July, he had another serious attack, during which he swallowed some paint.
1890	Vincent moved to Auvers, just outside Paris, where he became friendly with Dr Paul Gachet. On July 27, while out painting, he shot himself with a revolver. Gachet called Theo, who went immediately to his brother's bedside. Vincent died two days later on July 29.
1891	Theo died on January 25, six months after Vincent's death. He was eventually buried in the Auvers cemetery, next to his brother's grave.

◆ WHERE TO SEE WORKS BY VAN GOGH

Van Gogh's works can be found in museums and private collections throughout the world, including Russia, France, Germany, the United States and Japan. However, the two major collections of his works are in his native Holland: in the Rijksmuseum Vincent van Gogh in Amsterdam and the Rijksmuseum Kröller-Müller in Otterlo. Works that were kept for many years by Johanna Bonger, the wife of Theo van Gogh, and their son Vincent are also now housed in the Amsterdam museum. In addition to drawings and paintings, it exhibits family photographs and the letters that Vincent and Theo exchanged. A fair number of works by van Gogh can be found in other Dutch museums such as the Stedelijk Museum in Amsterdam, the Boymans-van Beuningen Museum in Rotterdam and the Haag Gemeentemuseum in The Hague. Outside Holland, the Musée d'Orsay in Paris, the Metropolitan Museum of Art in New York and the Chicago Art Institute also contain large collections of van Gogh's work.

AMSTERDAM

RIJKSMUSEUM VINCENT VAN GOGH
The Dutch government has devoted this museum entirely to the life and works of Vincent van Gogh. Here can be seen his portraits of the peasant people drawn and painted during the Nuenen period; his still lifes, such as *Still Life with a Plate of Lemons* and *Still Life with Bread*; the views of Paris, including *Vegetable Gardens in Montmartre* and *Boulevard de Clichy*; and many self-portraits. Other works found here include *Worshippers Leaving the Church at Nuenen*, *Gauguin's Chair*, a version of *The Potato Eaters* (the other is in Otterlo), *Skull with Lit Cigarette*, *The Langlois Bridge*, *Wheatfield with Crows*.

OTTERLO

RIJKSMUSEUM KRÖLLER-MÜLLER
This museum began with a large donation of works from a Dutch collector. Paintings here include some from the Nuenen period: a series showing weavers at their looms, the heads of Brabant peasant people, and the other version of *The Potato Eaters*. There are works from van Gogh's Paris period, such as *Moulin de la Galette*, *Windmills in Montmartre*, *Interior of a Restaurant*; works he painted in Arles, including *Pink Peach Tree in Blossom*, *The Langlois Bridge with Women Washing*, *Haystacks in Provence*, *Café Terrace at Night*; works from Saint-Rémy, such as *Landscape with Rising Moon* and a version of *L'Arlésienne*; and works produced in Auvers, such as *Landscape with Three Trees and Houses* and *Haystack on a Rainy Day*.

PARIS

MUSÉE D'ORSAY
The Musée d'Orsay has over twenty works by van Gogh, representing most stages of the artist's career. They include self-portraits from 1887 and 1889, *Starry Night on the Rhône*, a version of *Bedroom in Arles*, one of *L'Arlésienne* and the painting of *Dr Gachet's Garden at Auvers*.

NEW YORK

METROPOLITAN MUSEUM OF ART
The works exhibited here include *Peasant Woman Peeling Potatoes* and *Peasant Woman Seated in front of the Stove*, both painted in Nuenen in 1885; *Two Cut Sunflowers*, dated 1887; *Self-portrait with Straw Hat*, painted during the winter of 1887-88; one of the many portraits of Marie Ginoux and a portrait of Joseph Roulin, both from the Arles period.

CHICAGO

THE ART INSTITUTE
This museum houses another of van Gogh's self-portraits, painted in Paris during the spring of 1887, *Still Life with Grapes, Apples, Lemons and Pear*, *La Berceuse* (a portrait of Mme Roulin), a *View of the Park at Arles* and a version of *Bedroom in Arles*.

♦ LIST OF WORKS INCLUDED IN THIS BOOK

The works reproduced in this book are listed here, with (when known) their date, the technique used, their dimensions, the place where they are currently housed, and the number of the page on which they appear. The numbers in bold type refer to the credits on page 64.

Abbreviations:
w = whole; d = detail.
o/c oil on canvas
RVGA Rijksmuseum Vincent van Gogh, Amsterdam
RKMO Rijksmuseum Kröller-Müller, Otterlo
MOP Musée d'Orsay, Paris

Anquetin, Louis
1 *Portrait of Emile Bernard*, c.1887, crayon on paper, 71 x 59 cm (28 x 23 in) (RVGA) 34 w
Bernard, Emile
2 *Breton Women in the Fields*, 1888, o/c, 74 x 92 cm (29 x 36 in) (Private collection) 35 d; **3** *Bridges at Asnières*, 1887, o/c, 45.9 x 54.2 cm (18 x 21 in) (Museum of Modern Art, New York) 26 w; **4** *Self-portrait, to my Friend Vincent*, 1888, o/c, 46.5 x 55.5 cm (18 x 22 in) (RVGA) 35 w
Boldini, Giovanni
5 *Portrait of Giuseppe Verdi*, 1886, crayon on paper, 65 x 54 cm (26 x 21 in) (Galleria Nazionale di Arte Moderna, Rome) 22 w
Braque, Georges
6 *Landscape at La Ciotat*, 1906 (Galerie Beyeler, Basel) 39 w
Breton, Jules
7 *The Return of the Gleaners*, 1859, o/c (MOP) 11 d
Cézanne, Paul
8 *Dr Gachet in the Studio*, 1873, charcoal on paper (Louvre, Paris) 55 w; **9** *Dr Gachet's House at Auvers*, 1873, o/c, 46 x 37.5 cm (18 x 15 in) (MOP) 55 w; **10** *Mont Sainte-Victoire*, c.1887, o/c (Courtauld Institute Galleries, London) 39 w
Courbet, Gustave
11 *Burial at Ornans*, 1849-50, o/c, 314 x 663 cm (124 x 261 in) (MOP) 10 w; **12** *Spring Mating Season*, 1861, o/c, 355 x 507 cm (140 x 200 in) (MOP) 11 w; **13** *The Vercingetorix Oak*, 1864, o/c, 89 x 129 cm (35 x 51 in) (Pennsylvania Academy of Fine Arts, Philadelphia) 11 w
Daumier, Honoré
14 *The Laundress*, 1860, oil on board, 49 x 33.5 cm (19 x 13 in) (MOP) 10 w
Degas, Edgar
15 *The Tub*, 1886, o/c, 60 x 83 cm (24 x 33 in) (MOP) 23 w
Derain, André
16 *Landscape at Collioure*, 1905, o/c, 81.3 x 100.3 cm (32 x 39 in) (National Gallery of Art, Washington) 60 w, d
Gachet, Paul
17 *Portrait of Vincent on his Deathbed*, July 29, 1890, crayon (MOP) 55 w
Gauguin, Paul
18 *Jacob's Struggle with the Angel*, 1888, o/c, 74.4 x 93.1 cm (29 x 37 in) (National Gallery of Scotland, Edinburgh) 49 w;
19 *Nevermore*, 1894, o/c (Courtauld Institute Galleries, London) 49 w; **20** *Oviri*, 1894, pottery, 75 x 19 x 27 cm (30 x 7 x 11 in) (MOP) 48 w; **21** *Portrait of Van Gogh Painting Sunflowers*, 1888, o/c, 73 x 91 cm (29 x 36 in) (RVGA) 40 w; **22** *Self-portrait (Les Misérables)*, November 1888, o/c, 45 x 55 cm (18 x 22 in) (RVGA) 48 w; **23** *Self-portrait vase*, 1889, painted ceramic, height 19.3 cm (8 in) (Kunstindustrimuseet, Copenhagen); **24** *Vahine no te Tiare (Woman with Flower)*, 1891, o/c, 70 x 46 cm (28 x 18 in) (Ny Carlsberg Glyptotek, Copenhagen) 48 w; **25** *Vase with Breton Scenes*, 1887-88, painted ceramic, height 29 cm (11 in) (Musée Royaux d'Art et d'Histoire, Brussels) 48 w
Gogh, Vincent van
26 *The Alpilles with Olive Trees in the Foreground*, June 1889, o/c, 72.5 x 92 cm (29 x 36 in) (Whitney Collection, New York) 51 w; **27** *L'Arlésienne*, Jan-Feb 1890, o/c, 65 x 54 cm (26 x 21 in) (Museu de Arte, São Paulo) 45 w; **28** *Bedroom in Arles*, 1888, o/c, 72 x 90 cm (28 x 35 in) (RVGA) 46-47 w, d; **29** *Bedroom in Arles*, sketch in a letter to Theo, Oct 1888, pen and ink on paper, 13.5 x 21 cm (5 x 8 in) (RVGA) 46 w; **30** *La Berceuse (Madame Roulin)*, 1889 (Private collection) 44 w; **31** *Boulevard de Clichy*, 1887, o/c, 46.5 x 55 cm (18 x 22 in) (RVGA) 30-31 w, d; **32** *Boulevard de Clichy*, preparatory drawing, early 1887, pen, ink and colored chalks on paper, 38 x 52.5 cm (15 x 21 in) (RVGA) 30 w; **33** *Bridges at Asnières*, 1887, o/c, 52 x 65 cm (20 x 26 in) (Bührle Collection, Zurich) 26-27 w, d; **34** *Café Terrace at Night*, 1888, o/c, 81 x 65.5 cm (32 x 26 in) (RKMO) 51 w, d; **35** *Chair with Pipe*, Dec 1888, o/c (National Gallery, London) 47 w; **36** *The Church at Auvers*, June 1890, o/c, 94 x 74 cm (37 x 29 in) (MOP) 58-59 w, d; **37** *Courtyard of the Arles Hospital*, April 1889, o/c, 73 x 92 cm (29 x 36 in) (Oscar Reinhart Collection, Winterthur) 52 w; **38** *Cypresses*, June 1889, o/c, 93.3 x 74 cm (37 x 29 in) (Metropolitan Museum of Art, New York) 51 w; **39** *Dr Gachet's Garden in Auvers*, May 1890, o/c, 54 x 101 cm (21 x 40 in) (MOP) 54 w; **40** *Fishing Boats on the Beach of Saintes-Maries*, 1888, o/c, 65 x 85.1 cm (26 x 34 in) (RVGA) 43 w; **41** *Fourteen Sunflowers in a Vase*, Jan 1889, o/c, 95 x 73 cm (37 x 29 in) (RVGA) 43 w; **42** *The Garden of Daubigny's House*, July 1890, o/c, 53 x 103 cm (21 x 41 in) (Öffentliche Kunstsammlung, Basel) 58 w; **43** *La Guinguette*, Oct 1886, o/c (MOP) 56 w; **44** *Gauguin's Chair*, Dec 1888, o/c, 90.5 x 72.5 cm (36 x 29 in) (RVGA) 47 w; **45** *Harvest on the Plain of La Crau*, 1888, o/c, 73 x 92 cm (29 x 36 in) (RVGA) 38 w; **46** *Haystacks in Provence*, 1888, o/c, 73 x 92.5 cm (29 x 36 in) (RKMO) 43 w; **47** *Head of a Peasant Woman*, May-June 1885, black chalk on onionskin, 40 x 33 cm (16 x 13 in) (RVGA) 15 w; **48** *House of the Coal Merchant*, Nov 1878, pencil, pen and ink on paper, 14 x 14.5 cm (5 x 6 in) (RVGA) 12 w; **49** *Interior of a Restaurant*, 1887, o/c, 45.5 x 56.5 cm (18 x 22 in) (RKMO) 31 w, d; **50** *Irises*, 1889, o/c (Paul Getty Museum, Malibu) 57 w; **51** *The Italian Woman*, Dec 1887, o/c, 81 x 60 cm (32 x 24 in) (MOP) 34 w; **52** *The Langlois Bridge with Women Washing*, March 1888, o/c, 54 x 65 cm (21 x 26 in) (RKMO) 38 d; **53** Letter to Theo on Goupil headed notepaper, July 24, 1875 (RVGA) 20; **54** *Moulin de Blute-fin*, summer 1886, o/c, 38.5 x 46 cm (15 x 18 in) (Art Gallery and Museum, Glasgow) 32 w; **55** *La Mousmé*, July 1888, o/c, 74 x 60 cm (29 x 24 in) (National Gallery of Art, Washington) 45 w; **56** *Peasant Woman with Spade*, Aug 1885 (Barber Institute of Fine Arts, Birmingham) 15 w; **57** *Peasants Seated around a Table*, 1890, pencil and black chalk on paper, 22.5 x 30.5 cm (9 x 12 in) (RVGA) 14 w; **58** *Pink Peach Tree in Blossom (Souvenir de Mauve)*, 1888, o/c, 80.5 x 59.5 cm (32 x 23 in) (RKMO) 38 w; **59** *Portrait of Agostina Segatori at the Tambourin*, early 1887, o/c, 55.5 x 46.5 cm (22 x 18 in) (RVGA) 32 w; **60** *Portrait of the Art Dealer Alexander Reid*, 1887, o/c, 41 x 33 cm (16 x 13 in) (Art Gallery and Museum, Glasgow) 27 w; **61** *Portrait of Dr Félix Rey*, Jan 1889, o/c, 64 x 53 cm (25 x 21 in) (Pushkin Museum, Moscow) 52 w; **62** *Portrait of Dr Gachet*, June 1890, o/c, 67 x 56 cm (26 x 22 in) (Private collection) 54 w; **63** *Portrait of Dr Gachet*, June 1890, o/c, 68 x 57 cm (27 x 22 in) (MOP) 54-55 w, d; **64** *Portrait of Dr Gachet with Pipe*, May 1890, etching, 18 x 15 cm (7 x 6 in) (RKMO) 54 w; **65** *Portrait of Joseph Roulin*, July-Aug 1889, o/c, 81 x 65 cm (32 x 26 in) (Museum of Fine Arts, Boston) 44 w; **66** *Portrait of Père Tanguy*, autumn 1887, o/c, 65 x 51 cm (26 x 20 in) (Musée Rodin, Paris) 16 w; **67** *The Potato Eaters*, 1885, o/c, 81.5 x 114.5 cm (32 x 45 in) (RVGA) 14-15 w, d; **68** *The Potato Eaters*, 1885, lithograph, 26.5 x 30.5 cm (10 x 12 in) (RKMO) 14 w; **69** *The Public Garden in Place Lamartine with the Yellow House in the Background*, Sept 1888, pencil, quill, cane and ink on paper, 31.5 x 49.5 cm (12 x 19 in) (RVGA) 42 w; **70** *The Red Vineyard*, Nov 1888, o/c, 75 x 93 cm (30 x 37 in) (Pushkin Museum, Moscow) 56 w; **71** *Restaurant "La Sirène" at Asnières*, 1887, o/c, 54 x 65 cm (21 x 26 in) (MOP) 31 w; **72** *Return of the Miners*, 1880, 44.5 x 56 cm (18 x 22 in) (RKMO) 12 w; **73** *Riverbank at Asnières*, 1887, o/c, 49 x 65.5 cm (19 x 26 in) (RVGA) 27 w; **74** *Road with Steps in Auvers, with Figures*, May 1890, o/c, 49.8 x 70.1 cm (20 x 28 in) (Saint Louis Art Museum) 59 w; **75** *Self-portrait*, oil on paper, 34.2 x 25.5 cm (13 x 10 in) (RKMO) 36 w; **76** *Self-portrait*, 1889, o/c, 65 x 54 cm (26 x 21 in) (MOP) 37 w; **77** *Self-portrait in Front of the Easel*, 1888, o/c, 65.5 x 50.5 cm (26 x 20 in) (RVGA) 36-37 w, d; **78** *Self-portrait in Front of the Easel*, 1886, o/c, 46.5 x 38.5 cm (18 x 15 in) (RVGA) 36 w; **79** *Self-portrait with Bandaged Ear*, Jan 1889, o/c, 60 x 49 cm (24 x 19 in) (Courtauld Institute Galleries, London) 53 w; **80** *Self-portrait with Dark Hat*, 1886, o/c, 41.5 x 32.5 cm (41 x 13 in) (RVGA) 36 w; **81** *Self-portrait with Felt Hat*, 1887-88, o/c, 44 x 37.5 cm (17 x 15 in) (RVGA) 37 w; **82** *Self-portrait with Straw Hat and Pipe*, 1888, o/c on cardboard, 42 x 30 cm (17 x 12 in) (RVGA) 37 w; **83** *The Shoveller's Rest*, 1882 (Private collection) 13 w; **84** *Square in Ramsgate*, sketch in a letter to Theo, April 1876, pen and pencil on paper, 6.5 x 11 cm (2.5 x 4 in) (RVGA) 9 w; **85** *Starry Night*, 1889, o/c, 73.7 x 92.1 cm (29 x 36 in) (Museum of Modern Art, New York) 50-51 w, d; **86** *Starry Night*, 1889, drawing (Kunsthalle, Bremen) 50 w; **87** *Starry Night on the Rhône*, 1888, o/c, 72.5 x 92 cm (29 x 36 in) (MOP) 40 w, 51 d; **88** *Still Life with Bible*, 1885, o/c, 65 x 78 cm (26 x 31 in) (RVGA) 19 w; **89** *Still Life with Bottles*, 1884-85, o/c, 33 x 41 cm (13 x 16 in) (RKMO) 41 w; **90** *Still Life with Clock and Clog*, 1885, black chalk on paper, 27 x 18.5 cm (11 x 7 in) (RVGA) 18 w; **91** *Still Life with Clogs*, 1885, oil on board, 39 x 41.5 cm (15 x 16 in) (RKMO) 19 w, d; **92** *Still Life with Drawing Board*, Jan 1889, o/c, 50 x 64 cm (20 x 25 in) (RKMO) 41 w; **93** *Still Life with Plate of Lemons and Carafe*, 1887, o/c, 46.5 x 38.5 cm (18 x 14 in) (RVGA) 27 w, 41 d; **94** *Still Life with Straw Hat*, 1885, o/c, 36 x 53.5 cm (14 x 21 in) (RKMO) 18-19 w, d; **95** *The Town Hall at Auvers on 14 July*, 1890, o/c, 72 x 93 cm (28 x 37 in) (Private collection) 58 d; **96** *Two Self-portraits: Fragments of a Third*, 1887, pen, pencil and ink on onionskin, 31.6 x 24.1 cm (12 x 9 in) (RVGA) 36 w; **97** *Vegetable Gardens in Montmartre*, 1887, o/c, 96 x 120 cm (38 x 47 in) (Stedelijk Museum, Amsterdam) 30 w; **98** *View of the Port of Antwerp*, 1885, o/c, 20.5 x 27 cm (8 x 11 in) (RVGA) 17 w; **99** *Wheatfield with Crows*, Jul 1890, o/c, 50.3 x 103 cm (20 x 41 in) (RVGA) 59 w, 60 d; **100** *Worshippers Leaving the Church at Nuenen*, Jan 1884, o/c, 41.5 x 32 cm (16 x 13 in) (RVGA) 6 w; **101** *The Yellow House*, 1888, o/c, 72 x 91.5 cm (28 x 36 in) (RVGA) 42-43 w, d; **102** *The Yellow House*, Sept-Oct 1888, watercolor, 25.5 x 31.5 cm (10 x 12 in) (RVGA) 42 w
Guigou, Paul
103 *The Hills of Allauch near Marseille*, 1863 (Musée des Beaux-Arts, Marseille) 39 w
Hals, Frans
104 *Banquet of the Officers of the Militia Company of St George*, 1616 (Frans Halsmuseum, Haarlem) 19 d
Heckel, Erich
105 *Brickwork*, 1907, o/c, 68 x 86 cm (27 x 34 in) (Thyssen Foundation, Madrid) 61 w, d
Hiroshige, Ando
106 *The Bridge of Kyoto in the Light of the Moon*, print from *One Hundred Views of Edo*, 1856-59, 17 w
Israëls, Jozef
107 *Inside a Hovel*, 1890, o/c, 104 x 134 cm (41 x 53 in) (MOP) 15 d
Kirchner, Ernst Ludwig
108 *Woman in a Birch Wood*, 1906 (Thyssen Foundation, Madrid) 60 w
Luce, Maximilien
109 *Paris from Montmartre*, 1887, o/c, 65 x 54 cm (26 x 21 in) (Musée du Petit Palais, Geneva) 29 w, d
Manet, Edouard
110 *Portrait of Emile Zola*, 1868, o/c, 146 x 114 cm (57 x 45 in) (MOP) 10 d, 16 w
Matisse, Henri
111 *Landscape at Collioure*, 1905, o/c (Musée de l'Annonciade, Saint-Tropez) 39 w; **112** *View of Collioure*, 1905, 59 x 73 cm (23 x 29 in) (Hermitage, St Petersburg) 60 w
Maufra, Maxime
113 *Landscape at Pont-Aven*, 1890 (Musée des Beaux-Arts, Quimper) 49 w
Mauve, Anton
114 *The Seaweed Gatherer*, o/c, 51 x 71 cm (20 x 28 in) (MOP) 7 w
Millet, Jean-François
115 *The Gleaners*, 1857, o/c, 85.5 x 111 cm (34 x 44 in) (MOP) 11 w; **116** *Spring*, 1868-73, o/c, 131 x 88 cm (52 x 35 in) (MOP) 11 w
Monet, Claude
117 *Woman with Parasol*, 1886, o/c, 131 x 88 cm (52 x 35 in) (MOP) 22 d
Munch, Edvard
118 *Starry Night*, 1924-25, o/c, 120.5 x 100 cm (47 x 39 in) (Munch Museet, Oslo) 61 w
Nolde, Emil
119 *In the Wheat*, 1906, o/c, 65 x 82 cm (26 x 32 in) (Nolde Foundation, Seebüll) 61 w
Pissarro, Camille
120 *The Gleaners*, 1889, o/c, 65.5 x 81 cm (26 x 32 in) (Öffentliche Kunstsammlung, Basel) 22 d
Renoir, Pierre-Auguste
121 *The Great Bathers*, 1884-87, o/c, 118 x 170.5 cm (46 x 67 in) (Museum of Art, Philadelphia) 23 w
Rousseau, Henri (known as Le Douanier)
122 *Carnival Night*, 1886, o/c, 116 x 89 cm (46 x 35 in) (Museum of Art, Philadelphia) 23 d; **123** *A Riverbank*, 1886, o/c, 21 x 39 cm (8 x 15 in) (Private collection, Paris) 23 w; **124** *Self-portrait – Landscape*, 1889-90, o/c, 143 x 110.5 cm (56 x 44 in) (Národni Galerie, Prague) 25 d
Rousseau, Théodore
125 *Morning in the Forest of Fontainebleau*, 1850 (Wallace Collection, London) 11 w
Rubens, Peter Paul
126 *Self-portrait with his Wife, Isabella Brant*, 1609-10 (Alte Pinakothek, Munich) 17 w
Russell, John Peter
127 *Portrait of Van Gogh*, 1886, o/c, 60 x 45 cm (24 x 18 in) (RVGA) 37 w
Sérusier, Paul
128 *The Talisman*, 1888, o/c, 27 x 21 cm (11 x 8 in) (MOP) 49 d
Seurat, Georges
129 *The Circus*, 1890-91, o/c, 185.5 x 152.5 cm (73 x 60 in) (MOP) 33 w; **130** *The Circus Parade*, 1887-88, o/c, 99.7 x 150 cm (39 x 59 in) (Metropolitan Museum of Art, New York) 28 w, d; **131** *La Grande Jatte*, 1884-86, o/c, 207 x 308 cm (81 x 121 in) (Art Institute, Chicago) 23 w
Signac, Paul
132 *The Dining Room*, 1886-87, o/c, 89 x 115 cm (35 x 45 in) (RKMO) 23 d; **133** *The Lighthouse at Portrieux*, 1888 (Private collection) 29 w, d; **134** *Saint-Tropez – Storm*, 1895, o/c, 46 x 55 cm (18 x 21 in) (Musée de l'Annonciade, Saint-Tropez) 39 w
Toulouse-Lautrec, Henri de
135 *Carmen*, 1884, 52.8 x 40.8 cm (21 x 16 in) (Sterling and Francine Clark Art Institute, Williamstown, Massachusetts) 34 w; **136** *Moulin Rouge, La Goulue*, 1891, lithograph, 193 x 122 cm (76 x 48 in) (Victoria and Albert Museum, London) 33 w; **137** *Portrait of the Countess de Toulouse-Lautrec*, 1886-87 (Musée Lautrec, Albi) 34 w
Troyon, Constant
138 *The Pointer*, 1860 (Museum of Fine Arts, Boston) 10 w
Viesseux
139 *Portrait of Gustave Eiffel* (MOP) 24 w
Vlaminck, Maurice
140 *Houses and Trees*, 1906, o/c, 54.3 x 65.4 cm (21 x 26 in) (Metropolitan Museum of Art, New York) 61 w, d
Ward, Edward Matthew
141 *Portrait of Queen Victoria* (Forbes Magazine Collection, New York) 8 w

◆ INDEX

◆ CREDITS

The original and previously unpublished illustrations in this book may be reproduced only with the prior permission of Donati Giudici Associati, who hold the copyright.

ILLUSTRATIONS
Simone Boni, pp. 12-13, 24-25; Francesca D'Ottavi, pp. 4-5, 6-7, 8-9, 32-33, 34-35, 44-45; L. R. Galante, pp. 20-21, 52-53; Ivan Stalio, pp. 16-17, 40-41, 56-57.
COVER: L.R. Galante.
BACK COVER AND TITLE PAGE: Francesca D'Ottavi.

WORKS OF ART REPRODUCED
Alinari/Giraudon: 6, 27, 95, 103, 112, 123, 124, 137; Art Institute, Chicago: 131; Bridgeman Art Library: 2, 10, 13, 18, 19, 30, 34, 35, 37, 38, 50, 54, 55, 56, 60, 61, 62, 65, 70, 79, 83, 106, 108, 113, 120, 125, 136, 141; Bührle Collection, Zurich: 33; DoGi: 11, 115; Eric Lessing, Vienna: 24, 39, 66, 104, 118, 126, 129, 133; Galleria Nazionale d'Arte Moderna, Rome: 5; Kunsthalle, Bremen: 86; Kunstindustrimuseet, Copenhagen: 23; Metropolitan Museum of Art, New York: 130, 140; Musée du Petit Palais, Geneva: 109; Musée Royaux d'Art et d'Histoire, Brussels: 25; Museum of Art, Philadelphia: 121, 122; Museum of Fine Arts, Boston: 138; Museum of Modern Art, New York: 3, 85; National Gallery of Art, Washington: 16; Nolde Foundation, Seebüll: 119; Öffentliche Kunstsammlung, Basel: 42; Rijksmuseum Kröller-Müller, Otterlo: 46, 49, 52, 58, 64, 72, 75, 89, 91, 92, 94, 132; Rijksmuseum Vincent van Gogh (Van Gogh Foundation), Amsterdam: 1, 4, 21, 22, 28, 29, 31, 32, 40, 41, 44, 45, 47, 48, 53, 57, 59, 67, 68, 69, 73, 77, 78, 80, 81, 82, 84, 88, 90, 93, 96, 98, 99, 100, 101, 102, 127; RMN: 7, 8, 9, 12, 14, 15, 17, 20, 36, 43, 51, 63, 71, 76, 87, 107, 110, 111, 114, 116, 117, 128, 134, 139; Saint-Louis Art Museum, Saint-Louis: 74; Stedelijk Museum, Amsterdam: 97; Sterling and Francine Clark Art Institute, Williamstown, Massachusetts:135; Thyssen Foundation, Madrid: 105; Whitney Collection, New York: 26.
COVER (clockwise): Alinari/Giraudon: j, n; Bridgeman Art Library: d, q, r, u; Rijksmuseum Vincent van Gogh (Van Gogh Foundation), Amsterdam: a, b, e, g, i, k, l, p, s, v, w, x; Rijksmuseum Vincent van Gogh, Otterlo: o, t; RMN: c, f, h, m.

DOCUMENTS
Bridgeman Art Library: pp. 9, 25; © Collection Viollet: pp. 32, 56; Einaudi Archive: pp. 28c, 29tr; Harlingue-Viollet: pp. 33, 53, 54; Insel Archive: p. 53; ND-Viollet: p. 24; Rijksmuseum Vincent van Gogh (Van Gogh Foundation), Amsterdam: pp. 7cl, 7cr, 20t, 22c, 26b, 40b, 44t; Roger Viollet: p. 58.
BACK COVER: Rijksmuseum Vincent van Gogh (Van Gogh Foundation), Amsterdam.

Works by Heckel, Kirchner, Matisse, Munch, Nolde and Vlaminck have been reproduced with the authorization of the Società Italiana degli Autori ed Editori, 1996. © Succession Matisse by SIAE, 1996. © The Munch-Museum/The Munch-Ellingsen Group by SIAE, 1996.